MW01074743

Siblings All, Sign of the Times

The Social Teaching of Pope Francis

Cardinal Michael Czerny
and Christian Barone

Foreword by Pope Francis

Translated by Julian Paparella

ORBIS BOOKS
Maryknoll, New York 10545

Founded in 1970, Orbis Books endeavors to publish works that enlighten the mind, nourish the spirit, and challenge the conscience. The publishing arm of the Maryknoll Fathers and Brothers, Orbis seeks to explore the global dimensions of the Christian faith and mission, to invite dialogue with diverse cultures and religious traditions, and to serve the cause of reconciliation and peace. The books published reflect the views of their authors and do not represent the official position of the Maryknoll Society. To learn more about Maryknoll and Orbis Books, please visit our website at www.orbisbooks.com.

Library of Congress Cataloging-in-Publication Data

Names: Czerny, Michael, 1946- author. | Barone, Christian, 1982– author. | Paparella, Julian, translator.
Title: Siblings all, sign of the times : the social teaching of Pope Francis / Cardinal Michael Czerny and Christian Barone ; foreword by Pope Francis ; translated by Julian Paparella.
Other titles: Fraternità "segno dei tempi." English
Description: Maryknoll, NY : Orbis Books, 2022. | "Original edition, copyright 2021 by Libreria Editrice Vaticana, 00120 Città del Vaticano." | Includes bibliographical references and index. Identifiers: LCCN 2022026627 (print) | LCCN 2022026628 (ebook) | ISBN 9781626984820 (trade paperback) | ISBN 9781608339440 (epub)
Subjects: LCSH: Francis, Pope, 1936– | Christian sociology—Catholic authors.
Classification: LCC BX1378.7 .C9413 2022 (print) | LCC BX1378.7 (ebook) | DDC 261.8—dc23/eng/20220718
LC record available at https://lccn.loc.gov/2022026627
LC ebook record available at https://lccn.loc.gov/2022026628

From *Fratelli Tutti:*

> *Lord, Father of our human family,*
> *you created all human beings equal in dignity;*
> *pour forth into our hearts a fraternal spirit.*
>
> —*Francis,* "A Prayer to the Creator"

CONTENTS

Part II
Siblings All and Social Friendship: A "Sign of the Times"

FOREWORD

POPE FRANCIS

The heart of the Gospel is the proclamation of the Reign of God in the person of Jesus Himself, the Emmanuel, God-Is-With-Us. In Him, God brings His project of love for humanity to fulfillment, establishing His lordship over creatures and sowing the seed of divine life in human history, transforming it from within.

Certainly the Reign of God should not be identified or confused with some earthly or political achievement. Nor should it be envisioned as a purely interior reality, one that is merely personal and spiritual, or as a promise that concerns only the world to come. Instead, Christian faith lives by a fascinating and compelling *paradox*, a word very dear to the Jesuit theologian Henri de Lubac. It is what Jesus, forever joined with our flesh, is accomplishing here and now, opening us up to God the Father, bringing about an ongoing liberation in our lives, for in Him the Reign of God has already drawn near (Mark 1:12–15). At the same time, for as long as we exist in this flesh, God's Reign remains a promise, a deep yearning that we carry within ourselves, a cry that arises from a creation still marred by evil, one that suffers and groans until the day of its full liberation (Romans 8:19–24).

Therefore the Reign announced by Jesus is a living and dynamic reality. It invites us to conversion, asking our faith to emerge from the stasis of an individual religiosity or from its reduction to legalism. It wants our faith to become instead a continuous and restless searching for the Lord and His Word, one that calls us each to cooperate with the work of God in different situations of life and society. In different ways, often anonymous and silent, even in the history of our failures and our woundedness, the Reign of God is coming true in our hearts and in events happening around us. Like a small seed hidden in the earth (Matthew 13:31–32), like a bit of yeast that leavens the dough (Matthew 13:24–30), Jesus brings into our life story the signs of the new life He has come to initiate, asking us to work together with Him in this task of salvation. Every one of us can contribute to realizing the work of the Reign of God on earth, opening up spaces of salvation and liberation, sowing hope, challenging the deadly logics of egoism with the Gospel's spirit of siblings, dedicating ourselves in tenderness and solidarity for the benefit of our neighbors, especially the poorest.

We must never neutralize this social dimension of the Christian faith. As I mentioned in *Evangelii Gaudium*, the *kerygma* or proclamation of the Christian faith has an inherently social dimension. It invites us to build a society where the logic of the beatitudes triumphs, where a world of siblings all and of solidarity prevails. The God Who Is Love invites us in Jesus to live out the commandment of love for all as if we were siblings in a single actual family; with one and the same love, this God heals both our personal and social relationships, calling us to be peacemakers and builders of brother- and sisterhood among ourselves:

The Gospel is about the kingdom of God (Luke 4:43); it is about loving God who reigns in our world. To the extent

that He reigns within us, the life of society will be a setting for universal fraternity, justice, peace, and dignity.
Both Christian preaching and life, then, are meant to have
an impact on society. (*EG*, no. 180)

In this sense, caring for our Mother Earth and building a society
of solidarity as *fratelli tutti* or "siblings all" are not only *not*
foreign to our faith; they are concrete realizations of it.

This is the foundation of the Church's social teaching. It is
not just a simple social extension of Christian faith, but a reality
with a theological grounding: God's love for humanity and His
plan of love—embracing all as siblings—that He accomplishes
in human history through Jesus Christ, His Son, to whom all
believers are intimately united through the Holy Spirit.

I am grateful to Cardinal Michael Czerny and Fr. Christian
Barone, brothers in faith, for their contribution to the subject
and challenge of "siblings all." I am also grateful that this
book, while intended as a guide to the encyclical *Fratelli Tutti*,
endeavors to bring to light and make explicit the profound link
between the Church's current social teaching and the teachings
of the Second Vatican Council.

This link is not always noticed, at least not initially. I'll
try to explain why. The ecclesial climate of Latin America, in
which I was immersed first as a young Jesuit student and then in
ministry, had enthusiastically absorbed and taken possession of
the theological, ecclesial, and spiritual intuitions of the Council,
actualizing and enculturating them. For the youngest among us,
the Council became the horizon of our beliefs and of our ways
of speaking and acting. That is, it quickly became our ecclesial and pastoral ecosystem. But we didn't get into the habit
of quoting conciliar decrees, nor did we linger on speculative
reflections. The Council had simply entered our way of being
Christian and our way of being Church—and as life went on,
my intuitions, my perceptions, and my spirituality were quite
simply born out of what Vatican II taught. There wasn't much
need to quote the Council's documents.

Today, after many decades, we find ourselves in a world—and in a Church—deeply changed, and it is probably necessary to make more explicit the Second Vatican Council's key concepts, its theological and pastoral horizon, its topics, and its methods.

In the first part of their valuable book, Cardinal Michael and Fr. Christian help us with this. They read and interpret the social teaching in which I am engaged, bringing to light what is somewhat hidden between the lines—that is, the teaching of the Council as the fundamental basis and point of departure for my invitation to the Church and the whole world expressed in this ideal of "siblings all." It is one of the signs of the times that Vatican II brings to light, and the thing that our world—our common home, in which we are called to live as siblings—most needs.

In this connection, their book also has the merit of rereading, in today's world, the Council's intuition of an open Church in dialogue with the modern world. In the face of the questions and challenges of the modern world, Vatican II tried to respond with the breath of *Gaudium et Spes*; but today, as we follow the path marked out by the Council Fathers, we realize that there is a need not only for the Church to be in dialogue with the world, but, most of all, for it to put itself at the service of humanity, taking care of creation as well as announcing and working to realize a new universal sister- and brotherhood in which human relations are healed of egoism and violence and are founded instead on reciprocal love, welcome, and solidarity.

If this is what today's world is asking of us—especially in a society strongly marked by imbalances, injuries, and injustices—we realize that this, too, is in the spirit of the Council, which invites us to read and listen to the signs of human history.

This book by Cardinal Michael and Fr. Christian also has the merit of offering us a reflection on the methodology of postconciliar theology—a historical-theological-pastoral methodology in which human history is the site of God's Revelation. Here theology develops its orientation through reflection, and pastoral life incarnates theology in ecclesial and social praxis.

This is why papal teachings always need to be attentive to history, and why they require the contributions of theology.

Finally, I also want to applaud Cardinal Czerny for involving the young theologian Father Barone in this work. Their collaboration is fruitful—between a cardinal called to serve in the Holy See and be a pastoral guide, and a young fundamental theologian. This is an example of how study, reflection, and ecclesial experience can be joined, and it also indicates a new method: an official voice and a young voice, together. That is how we should always journey: the magisterium, theology, pastoral praxis, official leadership. Always together. Our bonds in the Church will be more credible if we too begin to feel like we are siblings all, *fratelli tutti,* and to live our respective ministries as a service to the Gospel, the building up of the Reign of God, and the care of our common home.

Francesco

Saint Peter's, Rome, October 3, 2021
First anniversary of *Fratelli Tutti*
—Translated by Griffin Oleynick

ABBREVIATIONS

AA   Decree on the Apostolate of the Laity *Apostolicam Actuositatem*, Second Vatican Council, November 18, 1965.

CA   Encyclical *Centesimus Annus*, John Paul II. September 1, 1991.

CiV   Encyclical *Caritas in Veritate*, Benedict XVI, June 29, 2009.

DCE   Encyclical *Deus Caritas Est,* Benedict XVI, December 25, 2005.

DH   Declaration on Religious Freedom *Dignitatis Humanae*, Second Vatican Council, December 7, 1965.

DI   Declaration on the Unicity and Salvific Universality of Christ and the Church *Dominus Iesus*, Congregation for the Doctrine of the Faith, August 6, 2000.

DiM   Encyclical *Dives in Misericordia,* John Paul II, November 30, 1980.

DV   Dogmatic Constitution on Divine Revelation *Dei Verbum*, Second Vatican Council, November 18, 1965.

EC   Apostolic Constitution *Episcopalis Communio,* Francis, September 15, 2018.

EG   Apostolic Exhortation *Evangelii Gaudium,* Francis, November 24, 2013.

EiE   Post-Synodal Exhortation *Ecclesia in Europa*, John Paul II, June 28, 2003.

EN   Apostolic Exhortation *Evangelii Nuntiandi*, Paul VI, December 8, 1975.

ES   Encyclical *Ecclesiam Suam*, Paul VI, August 6, 1964.

FC	Post-Synodal Apostolic Exhortation *Familiaris Consortio*, John Paul II, November 22, 1981.
FDA	*Final Document of the Synod for the Pan-Amazonian Region, "The Amazon: New Paths for the Church and for an Integral Ecology,"* Special Assembly of the Synod of Bishops for the Pan-Amazonian Region, October 26, 2019.
FT	Encyclical *Fratelli Tutti,* Francis, October 4, 2020.
GS	Pastoral Constitution on the Church in the World, *Gaudium et Spes*, Vatican Council II, December 7, 1965.
LE	Encyclical *Laborem Exercens*, John Paul II, September 14, 1981.
LG	Dogmatic Constitution on the Church *Lumen Gentium*, Second Vatican Council, November 21, 1964.
LS	Encyclical *Laudato Si'*, Francis, June 18, 2015.
MM	Encyclical *Mater et Magistra*, John XXIII, May 15, 1961.
NA	Statement on the Church's Relations with Non-Christian Religions *Nostra Aetate*, Second Vatican Council, October 28, 1965.
NmI	Apostolic Letter *Novo Millennio Ineunte*, John Paul II, January 6, 2001.
OA	Apostolic Letter *Octogesima Adveniens*, Paul VI, May 14, 1971.
OE	Decree on the Eastern Catholic Churches *Orientalium Ecclesiarum*, Second Vatican Council, November 21, 1964.
PC	Decree on the Renewal of Religious Life *Perfectae Caritatis*, Second Vatican Council, October 28, 1965.
PdV	Apostolic Exhortation *Pastores Dabo Vobis,* John Paul II, March 25, 1992.
PiT	Encyclical *Pacem in Terris,* John XXIII, April 11, 1963.
PO	Decree on the Ministry and Life of Priests *Presbyterorum Ordinis*, Second Vatican Council, December 7, 1965.

PP   Encyclical *Populorum Progressio,* Paul VI, March 26, 1967.

QA   Post-Synodal Apostolic Exhortation *Querida Amazonia,* Francis, February 12, 2020.

QAn   Encyclical *Quadragesimo Anno*, Pius XI, May 15, 1931.

RH   Encyclical *Redemptor Hominis,* John Paul II, March 2, 1979.

RM   Encyclical *Redemptoris Missio*, John Paul II, December 7, 1990.

SC   Constitution on the Sacred Liturgy *Sacrosanctum Concilium*, Second Vatican Council, December 4, 1963.

SrS   Encyclical *Sollicitudo Rei Socialis*, John Paul II, December 30, 1987.

UR   Decree on Ecumenism *Unitatis Redintegratio*, Second Vatican Council, November 21, 1964.

UuS   Encyclical *Ut Unum Sint,* John Paul II, May 25, 1995.

VD   Post-Synodal Apostolic Exhortation, *Verbum Domini*, Benedict XVI, September 30, 2010.

ACKNOWLEDGMENTS

Our special thanks are owed to Salvatore Rosa (Sicily) for the photo of the authors; Griffin Oleynick for first translation of the Holy Father's Foreword published by *Commonweal* in October 2021; Julian Paparella (Rome) for his fine translation from Italian to English, and for the revisions carried out by Andrew Boyd (Washington State), Richard Bernier (Montreal), Robert Czerny and Kevin Burns (Ottawa); the Libreria Editrice Vaticana, with appreciation for its cooperation in helping to make possible this English edition with Orbis Books.

INTRODUCTION

Our intention with this book is to introduce the 2021 Encyclical Letter of Pope Francis, significantly entitled *Fratelli Tutti,* which we translate as "Siblings All." In doing so, we first profile the work and teaching of the Argentinian pope—brought to Rome from the peripheries "almost from the ends of the earth"[1]—to highlight his continuity with the affirmations of the Second Vatican Council.

We will try to highlight the features that distinguish the "social" Magisterium of Pope Francis without claiming to be exhaustive or wanting to be apologetic.

Two preliminary observations may be useful in order to contextualize what we intend to develop in the course of this reflection.

The first premise is drawn from the text of *Dei Verbum,* in which the Council Fathers affirm that God has spoken to humanity with "deeds and words [*gestis verbisque*]" (*DV* 2). In describing the economy of Revelation, they wanted to emphasize the circularity (*perichoresis*) and the intimate connection between what God says and what God does.

It is important to note that they chose to give precedence to deeds, so as to emphasize that in the divine action it is the events of salvation history that "manifest and confirm the teaching and realities signified by the words" (*DV* 2).

We can apply this hermeneutic criterion to the pontificate of Pope Francis. In order to understand his Magisterium, it is not enough to refer to the speeches or documents promulgated in

---

[1] Pope Francis, *First Greeting of the Holy Father Pope Francis* (March 13, 2013).

the course of his papacy, but it is necessary to look at his actions. We need only think, for example, of the visit of Francis to the migrants who arrived on decrepit fishing boats or rubber dinghies in Lampedusa; of the meeting with women freed from the prostitution racket with the help of the *Comunità Papa Giovanni XXIII*; of the stop in Thailand to be close to the children who are victims of sex tourism; of the numerous apostolic trips in which he has been a "pilgrim" in various parts of the world; and also of the many gestures of hope expressed during and since the COVID-19 pandemic and all its upheaval.[2]

It is the concrete signs and actions that he has offered since the beginning of his Petrine ministry that illuminate the words that he has addressed during these years to Catholics, to Christians of other confessions, to the faithful of other religions, to believers and not, and to all people of good will.

The second premise is more general and concerns the way in which the Church has implemented the documents of the Councils that it has celebrated down through the centuries. History teaches us that not everything decreed by a Council is implemented in ecclesial practice in the same way and at the same time. We can easily see this by looking, for example, at the Constitutions promulgated by Vatican II; the liturgical reform, outlined by *Sacrosanctum Concilium*, was more readily accepted than the ecclesial renewal proposed by *Lumen Gentium*.

Over the past fifty years, the Church has seen a theological-pastoral "custom" take root that—de facto—has represented a truly selective interpretation of the Council. This shows us how, at least up until now, Vatican II has only been implemented in part and that much work still remains to be done.[3]

We can understand some of the fundamental choices of the Magisterium of Francis and his insistence on certain points of

----

[2] Pope Francis, "Why Are You Afraid? Have You No Faith?" Statio Orbis, March 27, 2020, *Our Sunday Visitor*, 2021.

[3] Cf. G. Lorizio, "Magistero scomodo: Vaticano II e papa Francesco," in *Dialoghi* 2 (2019): 9–14.

the Council as an attempt to follow up and find a way of implementing some of what remains unfinished: to implement those things that the Council documents indicate but which have not yet been fully integrated into the Church's living experience.

Among these, we can situate Francis's numerous reminders of the need for greater collegiality among bishops, a more significant role on the part of national episcopal conferences, and a renewal of the role played by the papacy. Also to be included are his continual references to various issues, such as the importance of women, the role of the laity, the preferential option for the poor, the dangers of clericalism, and the damage caused by the economy of exclusion.

The point here is not just to refer generally to some of the cornerstones of conciliar teaching, which Francis is obviously committed to promoting. We must also ask questions that aim to probe deeper into the link between the "Church that 'goes forth,'" which he has strongly desired, and the theological horizon traced by Vatican II. What elements enable us to see continuity in the teaching of the Church? What are the "interrupted pathways" of the Council that Francis wants the Church to rediscover in order to regain momentum today? In which direction is Francis trying to guide the future of the Church?

In order to answer these questions, it may be helpful to highlight four aspects of Francis's Magisterium that are not only deeply rooted in the transformation initiated by Vatican II, but that serve as an authentic way of interpreting the conciliar event itself.

Pastoral life as intrinsic to, not derivative of, doctrinal elaboration

Francis has made his own the most original intuition of John XXIII, which convinced him of the need to convene a council: prioritizing the good of souls and the need to respond to the necessities of the present time. Contrary to those who saw this pastoral life as something that followed doctrinal formulation, as if it were a practical application of principles formulated by deduction, John understood pastoral life as a constitutive and intrinsic dimension of doctrine.[4]

This same conviction is manifested in Pope Francis, who on several occasions has highlighted the need to overcome the "divorce" between theology and pastoral life, between faith and life.[5] Rather than being a "teacher" who reiterates the well-established principles of doctrine, Francis has chosen to present himself as a "pastor or shepherd" who accompanies his flock and guides it towards a more authentic fidelity to the Gospel. For this reason, since the first months of his pontificate, he has encouraged the Church to emerge from its withdrawal into itself and to stop speaking in a self-referential manner, because only by "going out and risking" does one gain concrete experience of what one is called to proclaim.[6]

This is why the mystery of the encounter with the Lord, true God and true man, is at the heart of the Magisterium of Francis. Recovering the kerygmatic nature of faith (*EG* 164) protects it

---

[4] Cf. G. Ruggieri, "Appunti per una teologia in Papa Roncalli," in *Papa Giovanni*, ed. G. Alberigo, Roma-Bari 1987, 245–271; cf. T. Citrini, "A proposito dell'indole pastorale del Magistero," in *Teologia* XV (1990) 130–149; cf. G. Alberigo, "Critères herméneutiques pour une histoire de Vatican II," in *À la veille du concile Vatican II. Vota et réactions en Europe et dans le catholicisme oriental*, ed. M. Lamberigts and C. Soeten, Leuven 1992, 12–23.

[5] As the Holy Father himself noted: "One of the main contributions of the Second Vatican Council was precisely seeking a way to overcome this divorce between theology and pastoral care, between faith and life. I dare say that the Council has revolutionized to some extent the status of theology—the believer's way of doing and thinking. I cannot forget the words of John XXIII who said in his opening address at the Council: "The substance of the ancient doctrine of the deposit of faith is one thing, and the way in which it is presented is another" (video message of Pope Francis to participants in an International Theological Congress held at the Pontifical Catholic University of Argentina, Buenos Aires, September 1–3, 2015).

[6] Cf. G. Costa, "La gioia del Vangelo: il segreto di papa Francesco," in *Aggiornamenti sociali* 65 (2014): 5–11.

from any theoretical meandering, bringing it back to the truth of that relationship with Christ that springs from the initial proclamation of the Gospel. Faith is not an ideology, but that concrete bond that we establish with the Lord and that impels us forward to meet others.[7] The establishment of this personal relationship within the Church gives rise to the desire to change one's life and the choice to bear joyful witness to Christ's love for the world.[8]

In this sense, both *Evangelii Gaudium* and *Laudato Si'* develop what Pope Paul VI had already expressed in *Evangelii Nuntiandi*. Stressing the importance of the joy of proclaiming the Gospel—recognizing in it a theological-pastoral criterion that guides ecclesial choices as well as the content of every evangelizing action—means reconnecting the Church to the foundational experience of Easter.[9]

The Church as the "People of God" on the way to salvation

The evocative image of the Church as the "People of God," taken from Scripture and renewed by *Lumen Gentium*, recurs frequently in the teaching of the post-conciliar popes. Francis, however, employs it in his own way. For him, "People of God" means recognizing in the encounter between the Gospel and cultures a further criterion for verifying the life of faith of the entire Catholic Church. The Church must allow itself to be challenged by the realities of the present and the challenges

---

[7] Cf. C. M. Martini, "Il seme, il lievito, piccolo gregge," in *La Civiltà cattolica* 1 (1999): 3–14.

[8] Cf. A. Spadaro, "*Evangelii Gaudium*. Radici, struttura e significato della prima Esortazione apostolica di papa Francesco," in *La Civiltà Cattolica* 164 (2013): 417–433.

[9] Cf. G. Benzi, "Il dinamismo dell'evangelizzazione: parola di Dio, annuncio, testimonianza," in M. Tagliaferri, *Teologia dell'evangelizzazione: Fondamenti e modelli a confronto*, EDB, Bologna 2014, 61–77.

that it faces, developing a response of contextualized faith that leads it to continually renew itself and express its faithfulness to Christ as time unfolds, generation after generation.[10]

If this were not the case, if the Church were to lose its consciousness of always being on the move, as a reality in the making, it would run the risk of absolutizing a given historical period and crystallizing itself in a particular form of the Church (*forma ecclesiae*).

Only a Church that recognizes itself as unique People of God can mature in its vocation to universality and be for everyone "the house of the Father, with doors always wide open" and "Mother with an open heart" (*EG* 46–47; *FT* 276).

For Francis it is necessary to rediscover "the spiritual savor of being a people" (*EG* 268–274), which means growing in the mature certainty and confessing with right intention that God wants the happiness of all human beings, that "no one is excluded from the joy brought by the Lord" (*EG* 3). In this perspective, we can perceive the challenges that the pope indicates for the Church in today's world, set out in detail in *Evangelii Gaudium*, as well as the first chapter of *Fratelli Tutti*: individualism, growth without integral development, the economy of exclusion, the prevalence of particular interests, inequality that generates violence, anthropological reduction-ism, and the lack of a shared understanding aimed at everyone being siblings everywhere, in universal solidarity and social friendship.

The close link between the proclamation of the Gospel and social commitment, between faith and justice, between joy and solidarity, shows how the essence of Christianity is summed up in charity. We can proclaim God's greatest truths to the world, but without that love that draws close and gives itself to the "injured" neighbor, in the image of the Good Samaritan, faith stops short at a merely theoretical level. Charity, on the other

---

[10] Cf. G. E. Rusconi, *La teologia narrativa di papa Francesco*, Laterza, Bari-Roma 2019, 89–90.

hand, is the antidote to any gnostic drifting, because it is never abstract.[11]

The attitude toward the poor, therefore, is a further discerning and decisive criterion for testing the unity of the People of God. It is not just a question of "helping the poor," but of recognizing that the poor are the measure of our conformity to Christ. For this reason, the poor evangelize us, they challenge us, and they call us back to the radicality of the demands of the Gospel.

The category of People of God in the Magisterium of Francis has prompted a further development of conciliar ecclesiology that is known as *inculturation of the faith*.[12] On the one hand, overcoming the strict identification of the Catholic Church with Western culture, as stated in *Gaudium et Spes*,[13] has made it possible to rethink the form of the Church (*forma ecclesiae*) as unity in difference, in the manner of trinitarian persons. At the same time, it is true that the direction taken by the post-conciliar Church has shown a certain resistance to implementing this principle.

For Francis, God's Revelation reverberates with every people, just as light refracts on the surface of a polyhedron (*EG* 235): every cultural identity is "flesh" in which the Word of God reveals the face of the Father.[14] The *Final Document of the Pan-Amazonian Synod* (*FDA*) states without hesitation that it is necessary to reject "any colonialist-style evangelization"

---

[11] Cf. G. Guccini, *Papa Francesco e la mondanità spirituale: una parola per consacrati e laici*, EDB, Bologna 2016.

[12] Cf. J. C. Scannone, "L'inculturazione nell'*Evangelii Gaudium*: chiavi di lettura," in *Evangelii Gaudium: il testo ci interroga. Chiavi di lettura, testimonianze e prospettive*, ed. H. M. Yáñez, GBP, Roma 2014, 159–170.

[13] We can cite the following affirmation of *GS* 42: "Since in virtue of her mission and nature she is bound to no particular form of human culture, nor to any political, economic or social system, the Church by her very universality can be a very close bond between diverse human communities and nations, provided these trust her and truly acknowledge her right to true freedom in fulfilling her mission."

[14] Cf. S. Noceti, *Chiesa, casa comune. Dal sinodo per l'Amazzonia una parola profetica*, EDB, Bologna 2020.

and that to proclaim the good news is to recognize that "seeds of the Word are already present in cultures" (*FDA* 55). Francis likewise explains that unity is not uniformity, but a "pluriform harmony" that assumes differences and values partiality, because "the whole is greater than the part, but it is also greater than the sum of its parts" (*FT* 78).

The care of our "common home"

Although the issue of safeguarding creation is not new to the Magisterium of the Church, thanks to both John Paul II and Benedict XVI, it is Pope Francis who stands out for his focus on the environment. Vatican II, looking at environmental issues, had already denounced how contemporary humanity relates to nature not as a wise steward, but thoughtlessly taking advantage to the point of impoverishing its resources and changing its equilibrium (*GS* 3). In this sense, the principles of solidarity and subsidiarity—which are two fundamental cornerstones of the social teaching of the Church[15]—should be seen as basic to a Gospel understanding of respect for creation.

However, with Francis's Encyclical *Laudato Si'*, we find ourselves before a novelty in the panorama of magisterial documents. Up until Francis, the environment had been dealt with as one theme among many in the teachings of the Church. Instead, Francis chose to dedicate a broad and complex text entirely to the environment, recognizing the inescapable, pressing relevance of the problem.[16] This is not a "green" encyclical but a magisterial teaching with an all-encompassing social emphasis: the fate of creation is inextricably and reciprocally linked to that of all humanity.

---

[15] Cf. Pontifical Council for Justice and Peace, *Compendium of the Social Doctrine of the Church*. LEV, Vatican City State, 2004, nn. 160, 187.

[16] Cf. *Abiterai la terra. Commento all'Enciclica "Laudato Si'"* con il testo integrale di papa Francesco, ed. G. Notarstefano, A.V.E., Roma 2015.

Francis's explicit denunciation of the "throwaway" mentality that generates a "culture of waste" and leads to the destruction of nature and the exploitation of more vulnerable persons and populations is intended to enable an ecological conscience to emerge that recovers a sense of limits, based on recognizing the value of the human person.

This document not only raises the alarm, but it also asks what can be done to "help us escape the spiral of self-destruction which currently engulfs us" (*LS* 163). Francis points out the need for worldwide *governance*, for an agreement that expresses common goals and establishes pathways to be followed together for the good of all.[17] Thus, the proposal of our all being siblings and of social friendship articulated by *Fratelli Tutti*, which goes beyond the limits imposed by particular ideologies and economic interests, is in continuity with and explicitly expresses what has already been outlined in *Laudato Si'*.

Dialogue as path, collaboration as method

Following the guidelines set out by Vatican II in the Decree *Unitatis Redintegratio* and the Declaration *Nostra Aetate*, Pope Francis has given a new impetus to the ecumenical movement and to interreligious dialogue.[18] From his point of view, when identity is strong, it does not fear encounter and dialogue; nor does it perceive the other as an enemy or a threat. On the other

---

[17] The Pontifical Council for Justice and Peace, in a Note in 2011, issued at the occasion of the G20 meeting in Cannes, had already put forward a proposal to set up a global authority that would operate in accordance with the principle of subsidiarity to help the most disadvantaged countries by guaranteeing an economic and financial policy that meets ethical and sustainable criteria. Cf. Pontifical Council for Justice and Peace, *Note on the "Reform of the International Financial System with a View toward a General Public Authority"* (October 24, 2011).

[18] Cf. W. Kasper, "Papa Francesco e le sfide dell'ecumenismo," in *Il Cristianesimo al tempo di Francesco*, ed. A. Riccardi, Laterza, Bari-Roma 2019, 15–36.

hand, avoiding confrontation expresses great fragility and deep insecurity. Those who have solid cultural and religious roots do not see the possibility of dialogue with those who are different as an impoverishment or a reduction, but rather take it as an opportunity to grow and mature in their own sense of belonging. These are the premises that Pope Francis lays out as the foundation of *Fratelli Tutti*, in which he invites us to recognize that religions "contribute significantly to building fraternity and defending justice in society" (*FT* 271).

When it comes to interreligious and ecumenical dialogue, it is Francis's gestures that precede and direct his words.

On the very day of his election, his choice to apply the seemingly modest title of Bishop of Rome to himself attracted the attention of non-Catholic Christians, particularly from the Orthodox Churches. Equally significant was the participation of Bartholomew, the Ecumenical Patriarch of Constantinople, in the inaugural liturgy of his Petrine ministry. This was truly an epochal event, since this invitation was without precedent in the history of the modern and contemporary Church. We can likewise think of the many visits, often informal and unplanned, that Francis has made during his travels: with the representatives of the Waldensian Church in Turin, to whom he expressed regret for the persecutions suffered in Italy; with the Pentecostal Christians in Caserta, with whose pastor he had developed cordial and friendly relations since before his election as pope; the meeting in Abu Dhabi with the Grand Imam Ahmad Al-Tayyeb in 2019; and the visit in Iraq to the Grand Ayatollah Sayyid Ali Al-Husaymi Al-Sistani in 2021. For the pope, it is not just a matter of getting to know others better, but of recognizing what the Spirit has sown in them as a gift for us too (*EG* 246).

The Magisterium of Pope Francis stands out for his wisdom and courage in focusing on the contextual aspect of the truth. He places a new emphasis on the "signs of the times" and underscores the "importance of reality" in the proclamation of the Gospel. This allows the Church to move toward rethinking its Magisterial posture, so that it may be more respectful of the diverse identities that make it up and more attentive to the sensibility expressed by other religions. It is not a question of limiting the usual claim of universality on the part of the Magisterium, but of understanding it in a different way.

Compared to his two immediate predecessors, Pope Francis shows a greater historical awareness of the progress of certain secular processes. By not merely denouncing the transformation of society that has taken place, he is able to propose a vision of the Church and Catholicism that is more consistent with historical reality. Giving up on tilting at the windmills of modernity is indispensable if the Church is to show renewed fidelity to the Gospel in today's world and to have an impact on the great social issues.

Looking to the future of the Church and humanity more than to the past gives the Magisterium of Francis a dynamic strength that can alarm and disorient. By constantly drawing attention to the poor, to migrants, and to the suffering of all kinds, Francis has often been misunderstood and accused of letting the social dimension prevail over the transcendent dimension of the faith. In reality, his appeals seem to be driven by a profound spiritual and eschatological tension. He is firmly convinced that "at the end of our life we will be judged on love, that is, on our concrete commitment to love and serve Jesus in our littlest and neediest brothers and sisters."[19] To recognize Christ in the face of the poor is to await the face-to-face encounter with our Risen Lord.

A note on translations and the text

A note on some of the terms in this book: first, *siblings*. We use this instead of the cumbersome phrase *brothers and sisters*. "Siblings all" is the proper equivalent of the encyclical title *Fratelli Tutti*, which has its origins in St. Francis of Assisi.

---

[19] Pope Francis, *Angelus on the Solemnity of Our Lord Jesus Christ, King of the Universe* (November 26, 2017).

Fratelli and related words continue to be understood widely in Latinate languages to denote both genders.

Accordingly, in this text *brothers and sisters* and *fraternity* are used only when a translation is being quoted. Otherwise, when referring to the all-important idea, reality and ideal, we use "all siblings" or sometimes, as in the book's title, echoing the Encyclical's title, "siblings all."

In Italian, *pastorale* is a noun (as well as adjective) designating all the Church's ministry or services. Since *pastoral* in English is only an adjective, we shall use "pastoral life" to indicate this most important dimension and reality.

In Italian, *storia* means both (past) history and (contemporary) events or lived reality. Since this latter meaning is not necessarily understood in the English words *story* or *narrative*, we shall use "contemporary history" to indicate the events, changes, and trends of the current times.

Finally, the Appendices serve as additional or supplementary reflections on the two parts of this book. They can also be read as an indirect but meaningful introduction to Part I on the teachings of Vatican II and to Part II on *Fratelli Tutti*.

PART I

THE SOCIAL TEACHING
OF POPE FRANCIS

1.

A TEACHING THAT CONTINUES
OR BREAKS WITH TRADITION?

Evangelii Gaudium features a synthesis—as well as a simplification—of the Church's social teaching with respect to *proclaiming the Kingdom of God*.[1] This new and decisive turning point hinges on understanding the social dimension of the Church's mission. With *Evangelii Gaudium*, this social dimension is no longer an addendum to the Gospel—as if it were simply an ulterior phase according to the adage "being precedes action/action flows from being" (*operari sequitur esse*). Rather, this social dimension is the Gospel's inner reality and is fully intrinsic. We can see this in the following dense passage of *Evangelii Gaudium*:

> The *kerygma* has a clear social content: at the very heart of the Gospel is life in community and engagement with others. The content of the first proclamation has an immediate moral implication centered on charity. (*EG* 177)

The essence of the social teaching of the Church is found in the "very heart of the Gospel." When it comes to proclaiming the Kingdom, this social dimension manifests itself as a choice to live together in community and to be concretely engaged in

---

[1] Cf. C. Theobald, "L'enseignement social de l'Église selon le pape François," *Nouvelle Revue Théologique* 138 (2016): 273–288.

serving others. In other words, the kerygmatic or missionary activity of the Church proceeds *outward*, since from the "heart of the Gospel" it moves toward the "heart of the people" (*EG* 273).

This shows how the *proclamation* and *reception* of the Gospel are not two distinct or independent phases but occur together as a single event that gives rise to bonds of sibling love (*EG* 179; 161). Proposing the Gospel and establishing relationships of charity and care are not separate endeavors; they are one and the same.

Pope Francis explains how our lack of attention to the poor and our reluctance in expressing tangible solidarity with our neighbors are related to our difficulty in building an authentic relationship of dialogue and familiarity with God (*EG* 187). Here, we can see a certain *principle of correspondence* between the authenticity of our relationship with God and our dedication to our siblings. This principle of correspondence guides us in our day-to-day commitments and offers us a criterion by which to evaluate our choices in the social, economic, political, environmental, and technological spheres.

The prominence of the *kerygma*'s "inescapable social dimension," according to *Evangelii Gaudium,* has elicited strong criticism from those who see it in discontinuity with the magisterial teaching of previous popes regarding the Church's social teaching. Particularly criticized is Pope Francis's statement that "neither the pope nor the Church have a monopoly on the interpretation of social realities or the proposal of solutions to contemporary problems" (*EG* 184).

This leads to the objection that the *prophetic* style of Pope Francis deviates from the more balanced tone that was previously adopted by the Magisterium. One example of this is Francis's severe denunciation of the wrongdoings that the "consumer society" perpetrates to the detriment of humanity, especially in the economic sphere. In this sense, Francis is accused of straying from the epistemological bases of the Church's social teaching and of being unbalanced in accentuating the "common good" to the detriment of the "rights of the individual."

Pope Francis is also criticized for not systematically attributing the imperfections and shortcomings of the social order to the reality of human sin. This could be seen as an apparent break with the tradition codified in the *Compendium of the Social Doctrine of the Church*.[2] The hermeneutics of social phenomena implemented by *Evangelii Gaudium* could be perceived as failing to take into account the established procedure of the Church's social teaching and as introducing—by means of the four criteria of discernment oriented toward social coexistence (*EG* 221)—an abstract content that is "alien" to the Church's social principles.[3]

These reservations about Francis's social Magisterium seem to lead back to the age-old debate concerning the question of *method* in theology. We need to address this problem and ask a specific question: Has Pope Francis introduced a "new" method or is his social Magisterium in continuity with the Tradition that preceded him?

To answer this question, it is helpful to uncover the historical depth of the issue, in order to show how two distinct approaches have emerged in the recent development of the social teaching of the Church. In the first part of this book, we will try to explain the difference and the coexistence between these two distinct perspectives by referring to the expression that has distinguished itself over time as a genuine stylistic feature of the Second Vatican Council: the *signs of the times*. The use of this expression in the magisterial reflection that followed

---

[2] Cf. G. Irrazábal, "Evangelii Gaudium la doctrina social de la Iglesia," *Revista Teología* 114 (2014): 131–143.

[3] This alludes to those principles that are aimed at guiding the Church's choices in the social sphere. The contents of these principles lead in various ways to the existence of a "priority" of spirit over matter, of the person over things, of ethics over technology, of work over capital, etc. Cf. Congregation for Catholic Education, *Guidelines for the Study and Teaching of the Church's Social Doctrine in the Formation of Priests*, Roma 1988, 44, 51.

Vatican II, almost like a litmus test, will make it possible to trace the distinctive features of the two different *methods*.

A new theological paradigm: Vatican II and taking responsibility before the world and history

On November 20, 1962, during the first session of Vatican II, the Council Fathers were called to vote on whether they would accept the preparatory schema "On the Sources of Revelation" (*De Fontibus Revelationis*) as the basis for their discussion on the sources of divine Revelation. The result of this vote demonstrated the Council Fathers' rejection of the schema[4] and the discussion in the Council assembly was suspended, allowing time to formulate a new draft. Clearly what was unfolding would decisively shape the outcome of the Council.[5] This was not, in fact, an isolated case. Ultimately, the Council Fathers raised objections concerning almost all the documents produced by the preparatory commissions, which had been coordinated by Cardinal Alfredo Ottaviani.[6]

What emerged from the assembly of Council Fathers, among bishops of various origins, formation, and cultural backgrounds,

---

[4] There were 1,368 votes against the schema and 882 in favor. However, according to the rules, a two-thirds majority was necessary not only to approve a text, but also to reject it. Despite the fact that 60 percent of the Council Fathers were in favor of reworking the draft, the text proposed by the preparatory commission was to remain as the basis for discussion. On November 21, John XXIII took matters into his own hands and decided that it was not necessary to reach a quorum. The will of the assembly was sufficiently clear to proceed with the withdrawal of the schema and the drafting of a new text. Cf. G. Martina, "La Chiesa in Italia," Edizioni Studium, Roma 1977, 90; cf. S. Schmidt, "Giovanni XXIII e il Segretariato per l'Unione dei cristiani," in *Cristianesimo nella Storia* 8 (1987): 95–117.

[5] Cf. G. Ruggieri, "Il primo. Il primo conflitto dottrinale," in G. Alberigo, *Storia del Concilio Vaticano II. Vol. II: La Formazione della coscienza conciliare*, Il Mulino, Bologna 1996, 259–294.

[6] Cf. Emmanuel-Marie, "Les quarante ans de la Constitution conciliaire Dei Verbum," in *Le Sel et la Terre* 55 (2005): 16–38.

was the awareness—both individual and collective—of the importance of the role that they were called to play in guiding the Church toward the long-awaited *aggiornamento* desired by Pope John XXIII.[7]

As often happens in moments of transition, even before focusing clearly on the new elements that need to be defined, the Council Fathers sensed what had to be rejected.[8] Thus they manifested the expectation by abandoning a *theological paradigm* that they considered unsuitable for the Church's understanding of itself, which had become excessively ahistorical. Instead, they sought a different narration of the faith that would speak in a more direct and accessible way to humanity and to the contemporary world.[9]

Gradually, the Council Fathers realized that the central issue in the task of rethinking doctrine in a "pastoral" key was the relationship between the Church and contemporary history. The most significant contribution that the Council could make to the Church of the twentieth century was rediscovering its

---

[7] Cf. R. De Mattei, *Il Concilio Vaticano II. Una storia mai scritta*, Lindau, Torino 2019, 254–265; cf. G. Alberigo, *Breve storia del Concilio Vaticano II*, Il Mulino, Bologna 2005, 47–52 (ET: *A Brief History of Vatican II* [Maryknoll, NY: Orbis Books, 2006]).

[8] The shift brought about by Vatican II can be described as an overcoming of the classical paradigm of "substance" in favor of a renewed emphasis on the category of "relationship." Substance is rethought vis à vis relationship, that is, the difference and otherness of the mystery of God who gives himself freely to humanity. Cf. J. C. Scannone, *La Teologia del Popolo: Radici teologiche di papa Francesco*, Queriniana, Brescia 2019, 136–137.

[9] Shortly before the opening of the Council, in a letter addressed to Father Karl Rahner, Father Chenu expressed his disappointment on having seen the preparatory *schemata*. He criticized its "strictly intellectualistic" character and the fact that they only sought to articulate "intra-theological errors." With reference to the schema *De Fontibus Revelationis*, Fr. Chenu noted the marked tendency to read divine Revelation without reference to history, "without mentioning the dramatic questions that men ask themselves, whether they are Christian or not, because of changes in the human condition, both exterior and interior, the likes of which human history has never seen before." M.-D. Chenu, "Vatican II Notebook," *Diario del Vaticano II. Note quotidiane al Concilio 1962–1963*, Il Mulino, Bologna 1996, 57.

own nature as the People of God journeying through time and history, gathered around the Word and the Eucharist, so that, freer from human conditioning, it could offer its own decisive contribution to the progress of humanity.

From its very first decisions, Vatican II reversed the direction and orientation that had marked the Church's posture toward modernity for more than four centuries. This change of course would overcome the reactionary mentality that had confined Catholics in a resigned state of victimhood and would mark the end of the so-called corporate role or regime of Christendom.

Instead, it was necessary for the Church to take upon itself the burden of confronting the great social changes that had occurred after the Second World War and, as *Pacem in Terris* indicated, to learn to recognize their relevance in the realization of the Kingdom of God. After reflecting on the nature of the Church in the Dogmatic Constitution *Lumen Gentium*, which highlighted what distinguished and differentiated its identity with respect to the "world," the Council Fathers were called to reflect on the way in which the Church would relate to the most serious contemporary problems in order to manifest itself as "sacrament of salvation" for humanity. The Church would embody its own path of following Christ (*sequela Christi*) within the contradictions of contemporary history, and it would seek its own adherence or fidelity to the Gospel through—and not in spite of—current human events. In this way, the Church would ably express its communal essence not by closing itself off in resentful self-defense, but by placing itself at the side of the peoples of the earth.

For these reasons, there was great interest around the drafting of *Gaudium et Spes*, the Pastoral Constitution with which Vatican II would prove capable of leading the Church into dialogue with humanity.[10] As the only document that was completely elaborated during the sessions of the Council, the

---

[10] Cf. L. Sartori, *La Chiesa nel mondo contemporaneo: introduzione alla Gaudium et Spes*, Messaggero, Padova 1995.

expectations placed upon *Gaudium et Spes* were so great that Yves Congar defined it in a radio interview as "the promised land of the Council."[11]

As the complicated history of Schema XIII shows, the initial stages of *Gaudium et Spes* date back to the first session of the Council in the autumn of 1962. It was subject to eight further revisions by various commissions, only to be voted on in the last working session of the Council, on December 6, 1965. It was approved the following day during the ninth solemn assembly, passing with 2,309 votes in favor and 75 against. In fact, its editing was only finalized on the evening before the Council solemnly closed on December 8.

As Joseph Ratzinger observed at the time, the importance of the Council's debate on Schema XIII consisted not only in recognizing the problems of the modern world and taking a step toward their solution, but in leaving open the invitation to continue reflecting on them. What distinguishes *Gaudium et Spes* is precisely the spirit or *ethos* that underlies its proposals: the courage with which the Council Fathers proposed a way of addressing the relationship between the Church and the world that in no way claimed to be exhaustive but instead anticipated further and deeper developments of the issues in question.[12]

The transition from an ahistorical paradigm to a historico-salvific reading of contemporary events also entailed a change of method. The text does not enunciate principles; nor does it put in the foreground the so-called presuppositions of faith (*preambula fidei*). Rather, to examine, question, and listen to the current socio-historical situation, the document takes as its sole reference the center of the faith (*centrum fidei*), the message of Jesus.

Of course, paying close attention to the context also modifies one's perception of the hearers to be addressed.

---

[11] Cf. H. Fesquet, *Diario del Concilio,* Mursia, Milano 1967, 392.

[12] Cf. J. Ratzinger, *Problemi e risultati del concilio Vaticano II*, Queriniana, Brescia 1967, 109–125. See J. Ratzinger, *Theological Highlights of Vatican II*, Paulist, 2009.

In fact, *Gaudium et Spes* wants to speak "not only to the members of the Church and all who invoke the name of Christ, but to the whole of humanity" (*GS* 2). In this renewed disposition toward universality, the Council also clarified the goal toward which to orient itself: "to offer to humanity the honest assistance of the Church in fostering the brotherhood of all men" (*GS* 3).

The Church-world relationship and Vatican II's "anthropological turn"

In *Lumen Gentium*, the Council introspectively examined the mystery of the Church, highlighting its communal and eschatological nature (*LG* 8–9, 48–51). This ecclesiological reflection, with its markedly doctrinal character, finds its natural complement in *Gaudium et Spes* (*GS* 2, 32, 40): from the Church as communion, constituted by the People of God, flows the dynamism of its mission in the world (*GS* 3). The adjective *pastoral,* which was used to describe the Pastoral Constitution *Gaudium et Spes*, had the precise purpose of illustrating how the salvific action of Christ on behalf of humankind unfolds through the mediation of the ecclesial community. Rather than assuming the divinely revealed Truth as a presupposition from which to deduce the guiding principles that would regulate ecclesial action in the world, *Gaudium et Spes* suggests rethinking the Church's missionary activity in relation to the questions men and women struggle to find answers to today. Special attention is to be paid to the concerns that emerge in every age and the questions of meaning that have always stirred in the depths of the human conscience. The Church is called to give reason for the hope dwelling within her by proclaiming the Gospel and giving the witness of charity.

Thus, *Gaudium et Spes* presents divine Revelation as above all an event of dialogue, as intrinsically an encounter and interchange. The revealed Truth, counting on the truth built into human consciousness, appeals to this innate predisposition to guide each one to welcome the mystery of God.[13] The "pastoral" essence or nature is defined as the desire to accompany men and women in the course of their life, through "the joys and hopes, the griefs and anxieties" (*GS* 1) that they experience, aware of the difficulties and challenges posed by the continuous changes and evolution of the realities in which they are immersed (*GS* 91).

Not a few critical voices were raised—then and now—against this perspective adopted by *Gaudium et Spes*, questioning its validity and accusing this conciliar document of producing a detrimental reduction of the universal validity of the Gospel message. Critics also point to the uneven way that the various topics are treated as evidence that the Pastoral Constitution never managed to duly integrate either the richness of the ecclesiological reflection proposed by *Lumen Gentium* or the sacramental perspective developed by *Sacrosanctum Concilium*. Yet it was precisely the methodological choice to describe the phenomena of contemporary reality that constitutes the progress made by *Gaudium et Spes* in comparison with previous socio-theological reflection. At the same time, it is said that this may have precluded the possibility of highlighting the dynamic function of Christian realities, giving the impression that they are only the result of human efforts.[14]

---

[13] Cf. B. Häring, "In luogo di conclusione: vie e prospettive nuove per il futuro," in *La Chiesa nel mondo di oggi. Studi e commenti intorno alla Costituzione pastorale Gaudium et Spes*, ed. G. Baraúna, Vallecchi, Florence 1966, 605–613.

[14] See, for example, Alberigo's thesis that the *Pastoral Constitution* did not achieve an adequate synthesis between divine Revelation and history to make it the unitary principle of the entire document. This is also demonstrated by the limited critical approach, which is lacking in its references to Christian sources and scriptural passages. The fault is attributed to a servile application of the schema *Ecclesia ad intra/ad extra* that was proposed by John XXIII in the opening speech of the Council. The splitting of Schema XIII to distinguish the path of the future *GS* from *LG* is said to have compromised its ecclesiological depth. The abrupt interruption of the work on *GS* due to the rapid closure of the Council is also said to have influenced the maturation of

However, a careful examination of the drafting process of Schema XIII shows that, in being referred from one commission to another, the text of the future *GS* was not considered insufficient because of its ecclesiological structure, but rather for its inadequate anthropological reflection. Indeed, in its treatment of the relationship between the Church and the world, an adequate reflection was lacking on the *world*, which should have been the formal object of the document.

In the period between the third and fourth sessions of the Council, Paul VI entrusted to a select committee of theologians the task of reworking the structure of Schema XIII.[15] The text was developed under the direction of Pierre Haubtmann and has gone down in history as the "Ariccia Draft."[16] This new draft added three new chapters to precede what had previously served as an introduction. These new chapters laid out the essential contents of a theological anthropology.[17]

The Pastoral Constitution was thus divided into two parts: the first part reflected on the human person in relation to temporal realities, to the world; the second part analyzed various

---

the text of the Pastoral Council, leaving it in an unfinished state of elaboration. Cf. G. Alberigo, "La Costituzione in rapporto al magistero globale del Concilio," in *La Chiesa nel mondo di oggi*, 179–191.

[15] Cf. G. Turbanti, *Un concilio per il mondo moderno. La redazione della costituzione pastorale Gaudium et Spes del Vaticano II*, Il Mulino, Bologna 2000.

[16] The central sub-commission entrusted the task of modifying Schema XIII to a drafting committee, which met under the direction of Pierre Haubtmann in Ariccia from January 31 to February 6, 1965. During these days of intense work, J. Danielou and K. Wojtyla outlined the theological reflection that was ultimately included in the final document, inspired by the patristic theology of the *imago Dei*. Cf. C. Moeller, *L'élaboration du schéma XIII. L'Église dans le monde de ce temps*, Casterman, Tournai 1967, 103–135.

[17] Cf. E. Schillebeeckx, "Fede Cristiana e aspettative dell'uomo," in *La Chiesa nel mondo contemporaneo. Commento alla Costituzione pastorale "Gaudium et Spes,"* Queriniana, Brescia 1972, 103–135.

aspects of contemporary life and human society, with special attention to certain urgent problems.

The recovery of the biblical-patristic doctrine of the image of God (*imago Dei*) (*GS* 12–13) made it possible to develop an anthropology that was narrative, articulated on the basis of the sequence "creation, sin, redemption." Human dignity and the necessity of Christ's grace converged in the presentation of the reality of sin (*GS* 16) within the framework of the tension between nature and grace, in keeping with the Augustinian-Thomistic tradition.[18] The Incarnation of the Word was identified as the hermeneutical principle that explains the fulfillment of creation as communion with God, through the final recapitulation of all things in Christ. The Incarnation of the Word likewise sheds light on the meaning of human life (*GS* 10) that the Church is called to reveal to all people (*GS* 41). Thus, by opening ourselves to faith, we can discover that the "natural" law that God has inscribed in our hearts is in fact innate and in conformity with the Gospel. With the help of the Holy Spirit, humanity can understand how the pedagogical work carried out by God in Revelation progressively guides it to fully embrace the truth.[19]

Gaudium et Spes applies the law of gradual progress and growing understanding of the truth to the human awareness that lets itself be increasingly enlightened by the mystery of Christ. At the same time, this same law of gradualness and progressive understanding of the truth is applied to the ecclesial mission of proclaiming the Gospel: listening, understanding, and interpreting the treasures hidden in cultures and the progress of science (*GS* 44), to test them against the Word of God. The aim is to

---

[18] J. Mouroux, "Situation et signification du Chapitre I: la dignité de la personne humaine," in *L'Église dans le monde de ce temps: constitution pastorale Gaudium et spes. Vol. 2: Commentaires*, Y. M.-J. Congar—M. Peuchmaurd (dir.), Cerf, Paris 1967, 229–253.

[19] Cf. S. Lyonnet, "I fondamenti biblici della costituzione," in *La Chiesa nel mondo di oggi*, 196–212.

understand the revealed message more deeply and to present it in a way that is even better suited to the men and women of today. This is precisely the pastoral mission that is entrusted to the Church.

Looking at history with the eyes of faith:
"Discerning the signs of the times"

In *Gaudium et Spes*, Vatican II affirmed that there is no opposition in principle between faith and modernity. This approach abandoned the judgmental attitude that had led the Church to stigmatize, almost a priori, every innovation as an "error" from which to protect itself. This prejudicial stance was the result of specific historical conditions and socio-political reasons from which the Church was now able to distance itself. Overcoming this position made it possible to lay the foundations for new efforts for the inculturation of Christian faith. This constructive approach was not, however, indicative of an uncritical or naive optimism. There was great awareness of the many questionable aspects and ambiguities that modernity brought with it, but the decision was made to take the path of communication and to engage in a dialogue based on trust. The Council wished to emphasize decisively that the communicative power of the Gospel manifests itself proportionally to the Church's ability to "express the message of Christ by making use of the concepts and languages of different peoples and philosophers." Indeed, the Council added that this effort of "existential" adaptation and mediation of the Word of God in ever-new forms, cultures, and languages is the "law of all evangelization" (*GS* 44).

Thus, following the logic of the Incarnation, the Church shows solidarity with the human family and, placing itself at humanity's service, opens itself to reflect on complex questions "about the current trend of the world, about the place and role of humanity in the universe, about the meaning of its individual and collective strivings, and about the ultimate destiny of reality and of humanity" (*GS* 3).

But the real novelty of *Gaudium et Spes* consists in presenting dialogue with the world as an exercise of self-awareness in the Church's identity. This dialogue is not exclusively aimed at making the proclamation of the Gospel more effective. Rather, it is necessary for grasping the signs of Christ's presence that emerge from contemporary history. Therefore, dialoguing with the world is not a question of carrying out a strategic marketing operation, or of embellishing the Gospel in order to capture the widest margin of consensus, even at the risk of compromising the message. On the contrary, being in dialogue with the world is a question of supporting the gradual and organic growth of the Church in the understanding of divine Revelation. Thus, progressing in the knowledge of the mystery of God depends on the ability of the Church community to immerse itself in contemporary history.

Engaging in dialogue with the world requires that the believer's perspective be renewed, that the "eyes of faith" be sharpened,[20] in order intelligently to see reality and grasp the social transformations and changes taking place in humanity. Such dialogue must also reflect on their deeper significance, to see if they serve as markers of the Kingdom of God approaching. This is what the Pastoral Constitution presents as the Church's permanent duty of "*scrutinizing the signs of the times*" (*GS* 4).

---

[20] Rousselot's thought, through de Lubac's contribution, reached Vatican II. Faith springs from God's act of love that, by transforming the human person internally, enables that person to look at reality in a new way, in the manner of Jesus, with Jesus's eyes. Rousselot wrote: "In the act of faith, just as love is necessary for knowledge, so too knowledge is necessary for love. Love, which is free adhesion to the Supreme Good, gives us new eyes." This is the perspective adopted by *Gaudium et Spes*: the gaze of the believer is a dynamism in continuous growth, because as we increase our knowledge of things, of the world, of experience, this deepens and clarifies our relationship with Christ.

The expression *signs of the times* appears only three times in *Gaudium et Spes* and another four times in other conciliar documents,[21] but its meaning is prevalent in various ways. *Signs of the times* can have a twofold meaning: in a broad sense, it indicates the phenomena that characterize a given era (this is the sociological perspective); in a more particular sense, it refers to the results of the process of discernment through which the Church assesses contemporary history in the light of faith (this is the theological perspective).[22]

Examining *Gaudium et Spes* as a whole, it can be argued that both meanings were intended by the Council Fathers, though the first is always subordinated to the second. The Council set forth, as the Church's "permanent duty," the exercise of interpreting contemporary historical events in such a way that the theological perspective presupposes the phenomenological or sociological point of view.

M.-D. Chenu defined this combination of perspectives as an *inductive method*. This way of proceeding features perceiving the questions of meaning that are posed by men and women in a given age in order to give greater prominence to the Revelation of the mystery of God in history.[23] The category "signs of the times" thus acquired its own significance. It aims at recognizing history—not only the past but especially

---

[21] *GS* 4, 11, 44; *PO* 9; *AA* 14; *UR* 4.

[22] Cf. J.-F. Chiron, "Discernement des signes des temps ou application de la doctrine sociale de l'Église? Évolutions et diversité des interprétations dans le magistère postconciliaire," in *Théophilyon* XVIII-1 (2013), 45–88. These two tendencies already emerged in the preparatory discussion of the text of the document in the confrontation between M. G. McGrath and J. Danielou: the former argued for giving the expression a sociological meaning, the latter for giving it a more theological value. Cf. G. Turbanti, *Un Concilio per il mondo moderno. La redazione della costituzione pastorale "Gaudium et Spes" del Vaticano II*, Il Mulino, Bologna 2000, 373–382.

[23] Cf. M.-D. Chenu, *La Chiesa nel mondo. I segni dei tempi*, Vita e Pensiero, Milano 1965, 9–39; cf. A. Cortesi, *Marie-Dominique Chenu. Un percorso teologico*, Nerbini, Firenze 2007, 127–157.

contemporary—as an effective source of theology (*locus theologicus*).[24]

The expression *signs of the times* in Protestant literature was understood with a prevalently apocalyptic meaning. However, in the Catholic sphere a messianic interpretation prevailed. In this sense, the signs of the times are a sign of the One who is coming, and they point to our duty to seek the traces of God's coming among us through peoples' concrete experiences in contemporary history.

As Yves Congar explained, *Gaudium et Spes* expressed the conviction that the Church should allow itself to be questioned by the movements and problems of the world. This would enable the Church to rethink its own faith in the particular context and circumstances of the events through which the Spirit is calling out in today's world.[25] In other words, with the signs of the times one is assuming a way of living and working (*modus operandi et vivendi*)—a stable attitude of the Church—as a way of looking at reality that is capable of judging the unfolding contemporary history with evangelical wisdom.

The People of God: Exercising evangelical discernment through the faithful's sense of the faith

The inductive method proposed in *Gaudium et Spes* 4 unfolds in three stages: *scrutinizing* the signs of the times;

---

[24] Cf. G. Ruggieri, *La verità crocifissa. Il pensiero cristiano di fronte all'alterità*, Carocci, Roma 2007, 81–114.

[25] Cf. Y. Congar, "Bloc-notes sur la Concile." The meaning attributed to the expression "signs of the times" by Congar can also be deduced from numerous passages in his writings: "It is required that the *aggiornamento* of the Council does not stop at the adaptation of the forms of ecclesial life but goes as far as a total evangelical radicalism and the invention, by the Church, of a way of being, of speaking, of committing oneself, which responds to the demands of a total evangelical service to the world" (Y. Congar, *Vera e falsa riforma della Chiesa*, Jaca Book, Milano 1950, 12).

interpreting them in the light of the Gospel; and *responding* to questions of meaning. It should be emphasized that the Council attributes this activity of discernment to the entire People of God in the exercise of their faith in Christ Jesus.

> The People of God believes that it is led by the Lord's Spirit, Who fills the earth. Motivated by this faith, it labors to decipher authentic signs of God's presence and purpose in the happenings, needs and desires in which this People has a part along with other men of our age. For faith throws a new light on everything, manifests God's design for man's total vocation, and thus directs the mind to solutions which are fully human. (*GS* 11)

In referring to the Church in its totality, the Council affirms that discernment in contemporary history is an activity that arises as a particular form of exercising the faithful's sense of the faith (*sensus fidei fidelium*). This sense is the supernatural instinct for the truth manifested in the totality of the faithful,[26] which allows them to judge in a spontaneous manner—being one by nature (connatural) with the object of faith—the authenticity of doctrine, and so to converge in adherence to it or to an element of Christian praxis.[27] Since this convergence or consensus of the faithful (*consensus fidelium*) constitutes an indispensable criterion of discernment for the life of the Church, it is likewise a resource for its mission of evangelization. By affirming that the anointing of the Spirit is manifested in the sense of faith (*sensus fidei*) of the totality of the faithful (*LG* 12), the Council wished to reaffirm that Christ exercises his

---

[26]It is compared to an instinct because it is not primarily the result of rational deliberation, but rather takes the form of spontaneous and natural knowledge, a kind of perception (*aisthêsis*).

[27]*LG* 12 states: "The entire body of the faithful, anointed as they are by the Holy One (cf. Jn 2:20, 27) cannot err in matters of belief. They manifest this special property by means of the whole peoples' supernatural discernment in matters of faith when from the bishops down to the last of the lay faithful they show universal agreement in matters of faith and morals."

prophetic office in the Church not only through the hierarchy, but also through the laity. In recognizing an effective autonomy of the laity in their temporal engagements and activities, great responsibility is attributed to their task of bringing together "human, domestic, professional, social and technical enterprises by gathering them into one vital synthesis with religious values, under whose supreme direction all things are harmonized unto God's glory" (*GS* 43).

Beyond the faithful's sense of faith, beyond the emphasis on the subject, that is the whole People of God in the diversity of charisms, there is an emphasis on the faith. The faith not only confers the power to discern "God's plan" amid the current events of the world, but is also the formal point of view from which to perceive the needs and aspirations of each generation.

The exercise of faith implies attaining a sensibility and intuition in this regard. By grasping the inclinations expressed by humanity in a given cultural context, one can perceive in them that anticipation or expectation of grace that constitutes a true sign of God's presence.

Gaudium et Spes thus affirms that contemporary history is not only the objective of ecclesial action but claims that this unfolding history presents itself to the Church as an inexhaustible source of riches:

> Just as it is in the world's interest to acknowledge the Church as an historical reality, and to recognize her good influence, so the Church herself knows how richly she has profited by the history and development of humanity. The experience of past ages, the progress of the sciences, and the treasures hidden in the various forms of human culture, by all of which the nature of man himself is more clearly revealed and new roads to truth are opened, these profit the Church, too. (*GS* 44)

In particular, the Council perceived that in the recent history of humankind, the scientific mentality had changed everyone's view of the world, substantially influencing ordinary people's way of thinking. The contribution of scientific disciplines had introduced categories and meanings that could no longer be ignored if one wanted to proclaim the Gospel credibly.

Therefore, in reaffirming that faith is nourished by reading the narrative of the times or contemporary history, the text focuses on what is the proper role of the Church.

> It is the task of the entire People of God, especially pastors and theologians, to hear, distinguish and interpret the many voices of our age, and to judge them in the light of the divine word, so that revealed truth can always be more deeply penetrated, better understood, and set forth to greater advantage.
>
> Since the Church has a visible and social structure as a sign of her unity in Christ, she can and ought to be enriched by the development of human social life, not that there is any lack in the constitution given her by Christ, but that she can understand it more penetratingly, express it better, and adjust it more successfully to our times. (*GS* 44)

The Council Fathers pointed out that discernment always implies an effort to extract from the "languages" of the day those expressions of human values that can help to illustrate the truth of Revelation in Christ. As a result, some interpret these words as an invitation to "purify" the cultural expression of a given society. This exegesis of *Gaudium et Spes* 44 would imply a negative reading of cultural-historical expressions and the conviction that only the Church possesses the "right" criterion by which to judge them. The discernment would imply the Church's relationship of authority with every cultural expression and claim for itself a stance of vigilance.

But this interpretation of the Pastoral Constitution, while possible and not entirely illegitimate, in fact runs counter to the aspirations of the document itself, which calls for the possibility of dialogue with the contemporary world.

In fact, the Church's participation in the events of the world, taking part in them "along with other men of our age" (*GS* 11), characterizes its presence in a "synodal" way. The Church shares contemporary history with the rest of humanity, it is immersed and involved in temporal events, and its activity of discernment is not aimed at expressing a condemnation of the world, but at facilitating the world's encounter with God. This is not a Church that observes the world from the outside, but one that allows itself to be stirred by what happens in the world in its constant effort to discover "God's plan" for all.

By faith, we already know what this *plan* is, namely, God's universal salvific will for humanity. But we do not know precisely *how* it will unfold, how it will come about. We know the goal, the final recapitulation in Christ, but the current pilgrim condition—suspended between the *already* and the *not yet*—obliges the People of God, which is the Church, to pay attention to contemporary history, to the "signs" that are manifested in time, as if traces of footsteps by which the Church is led to salvation. It is therefore necessary to note the strong eschatological connotation of the conciliar affirmation, which expresses the Council's determination to observe contemporary human history as it moves toward its ultimate fulfillment.

2.

AFTER THE COUNCIL, TWO APPROACHES TO SOCIAL QUESTIONS EMERGE

A quick glance at the historico-theological debates that in recent decades have addressed the questions and problems of the path taken by the Catholic Church in the aftermath of Vatican II clearly shows how difficult it is to handle the interpretation of continuity-and/or-discontinuity in the analysis of complex events, as in this case of an overall evaluation of the pronouncements of a Council. There is a constant risk of generalization and oversimplification.

At the same time, the dialectic between continuity and reform has been constant throughout the history of the Church. Looking to history provides insights into the turning points and epochal transitions that have marked the progress of the Church through the ages.

Pope Francis has spoken about the style and meaning of his own "reform." He explains that what moves him in the direction of certain choices is the intention to base change on fidelity to the deposit of faith (*depositum fidei*) and to the Tradition. The question, however, is establishing how to interpret the concept of *Traditio* and to specify its function in relation to the needs of the present.

As Francis himself said, the appreciation of history is an indispensable prerequisite for building a solid future, but reference to the past must not be a pretext for inertia:

Appealing to memory is not the same as being anchored in self-preservation, but instead to evoke the life and vitality of an ongoing process. Memory is not static, but dynamic. By its very nature, it implies movement. Nor is tradition static; it too is dynamic, as that great man [Gustav Mahler, taking up a metaphor used by Jean Jaurès] used to say: tradition is the guarantee of the future and not a container of ashes.[1]

In these words we see a well-tuned hermeneutics of Tradition, revealing how it can be transmitted thanks also to discontinuity, without necessarily entailing a break with the past. On the contrary, renewal can appear as the only way to truly serve Tradition and preserve its essential contents.

In this chapter, we will try to show how the Magisterium of Pope Francis is characterized by his taking up again the inductive method introduced by Vatican II, in continuity with the teaching of Saint John XXIII and Saint Paul VI, who promoted this approach. At the same time, Francis's continuity with his immediate predecessors, Saint John Paul II and Benedict XVI, does not seem to show so much in terms of method, but in the emphasis on certain themes and perspectives toward which to orient the future of the Church.

John XXIII and Paul VI:
The Church immersed in the "human" history of salvation

The posture of dialogue with which the Church is called to "see, discern, and act" in the world was defined as ecclesial practice by the Second Vatican Council, but it found an authoritative precedent in the Magisterium of John XXIII.

On several occasions, Pope John expressed a strong desire for the Church to engage in the quest for an effective renewal

---

[1] Pope Francis, *Christmas Greetings of the Holy Father to the Roman Curia*, December 21, 2019.

or updating (*aggiornamento*). The term was not intended to describe a process of adapting the Church to the needs of the present time, but rather to indicate a change in mentality so as to rethink its presence in the world. *Pastoral life* has to be understood as an intrinsic requirement of expressing doctrine or teaching, because only by encountering people's expectations and hopes would one succeed in transmitting the living substance of the Gospel in today's world.

In this sense, Pope John rejected the negative conception of contemporary history that had characterized modern apologetics, which denounced the progressive deterioration of humankind over the centuries as a result of sin. Instead, he tried to ensure that the Church would encounter the positive events in contemporary history as "good" signs to welcome with joy.

In his Encyclical *Mater et Magistra*, John XXIII refers to the most significant social and political changes of recent history. He mentions and approves events such as disarmament, the promotion of human rights, economic development, and scientific innovation. It would be extremely reductive to claim that he merely offered the Church an optimistic view of history to correct its defeatist attitude and its habit of condemning progress. Rather, his aim was to give theology a new direction. Instead of drawing its own understanding of the economy of salvation from abstract premises, theology would have to develop from a continual encounter with history, manifesting its capacity to show the world that the Kingdom of God is a dynamic event and reality.

We can see how the category "signs of the times" is not only consistent with that of renewal or *aggiornamento* and of "pastoral life," it also informed the entire magisterium of John XXIII. The four chapters that make up *Pacem in Terris* can be read as evangelical discernment made explicit and an application of the *inductive method*. The economic and social rise of the working classes, the entry of women into public life, the end of colonialism, equality between peoples, and the commitment to build a lasting world peace all become meaningful signposts that nourish the awareness with which the Church understands its mission and its vocation at the service of all people and not just of Christians.[2]

Paul VI inherited this awareness of the "signs of the times" from John XXIII and the Second Vatican Council, but he also perceived its ambivalence. His Magisterium sought to clarify the category, so that it would not be reduced to a mere recording of "facts," but that in it one would perceive that abundant "more" that signals God at work. To say that the People of God is immersed in the present means, at the same time, to affirm that it is involved in the contemporary history of humanity oriented toward salvation.[3]

In this sense, for Paul VI, the synchronic reading of the epochal events of today's history must be completed with a diachronic one. Taken together, these two approaches avoid the risk of falling into "charismatic prophetism" or into the myopia caused by merely observing "phenomena." Only if our view or gaze on the present is capable of projecting into the future can the signs of the times inform and orient the action of the Church, for "the world becomes a book for us." Thus the Christian must exercise discernment and watchfulness, so that the signs become "news of an immanent Providence" and "clues" to the hidden action of the Kingdom of God.[4]

In his Encyclical *Ecclesiam Suam* (1962), Pope Paul declares that reading the "signs of the times" constitutes "a stimulus to the Church to increase its ever-growing vitality," linked with the awareness that perfection does not "consist in rigidly adhering to the methods adopted by the Church in the past and refusing to countenance the practical measures commonly thought to be in accord with the character of our time" (*ES* 50).

---

[2] Cf. P. Sacrofani, *Segni dei tempi. Segni dell'amore*, Paoline, Milano 2002, 24–27.

[3] Cf. C. Stercal, *Paolo VI. Un ritratto spirituale*, Edizioni Studium Roma, Brescia-Roma 2016; cf. G. Garancini, "Il senso di Paolo VI per la storia. 'Il mondo per noi diventa libro,'" in *A 50 anni dalla Populorum Progressio. Paolo VI, il papa della modernità, giustizia tra i popoli e l'amore per l'Italia*, ed. C. Cardia and R. Benigni, RomaTre-Press, Roma 2018, 99–114.

[4] Pope Paul VI, *General Audience,* Wednesday, April 16, 1969.

The Church is indeed called, in its dynamics and structures of evangelization, to be docile to that change, which is generated by the action of the Spirit, so that the world may grasp the current real relevance of Christ's salvation.

Pope Paul VI would later return, in *Evangelii Nuntiandi*, to emphasize the role of the Holy Spirit in evangelization that springs from attention and commitment to contemporary history: "Through the Holy Spirit the Gospel penetrates to the heart of the world, for it is He who causes people to discern the signs of the times—signs willed by God—which evangelization reveals and puts to use within history" (*EN* 75). The Spirit helps to align contemporary history and the Gospel, acting as mediator and guarantor, supporting the Church in its reading of the "signs" and on this basis orienting itself to the mission.

But it is in *Octogesima Adveniens* that Pope Paul shows his desire to follow up on and develop the inductive method proposed by *Gaudium et Spes*, carefully articulating a reflection on the discernment of the "signs of the times" (*OA* 8–41) as a tool for reading social realities.[5] He affirms:

It is up to the Christian communities to analyze with objectivity the situation, which is proper to their own country, to shed on it the light of the Gospel's unalterable words and to draw principles of reflection, norms of judgment and directives for action from the social teaching of the Church. This social teaching has been worked out in the course of history and notably, in this industrial era, since the historic date of the message of Pope Leo XIII on "the condition of the workers," and it is an honor and joy for us to celebrate today the anniversary of that message. It is up to these Christian communities, with the help of the Holy Spirit, in communion with the bishops who hold responsibility and in dialogue with other Christian brethren and all men of goodwill, to discern the options

---

[5] Likewise, in *Populorum Progressio* (1967), Paul VI explicitly cites *GS* 4, pointing to the inductive method "see, discern, act" (*PP* 13).

and commitments which are called for in order to bring about the social, political and economic changes seen in many cases to be urgently needed. (*OA* 4)

The apostolic letter suggests tackling problems not within a deductive framework derived from doctrinal sources, but through an inductive analysis of events; by truly relying on the assistance of the Spirit, such analysis can identify new paths and courageous choices. Thus there is no single, universal solution to the difficulties brought about by today's social realities, but each Christian community must take up the task of finding adequate responses to the complexities of its own specific context.

The action of the Church in view of the transformations necessary to renew the face of humanity presupposes that the main actors of the Church's presence in society are the members who together form a local church.

They will have to discern by keeping in mind that the criteria of reference are the Gospel and the Church's social teaching, while also leaving room for the creativity of the Holy Spirit. In this way, the inductive method as spelled out by Catholic Action in its three steps of see-judge-act needs also to be shaped by magisterial social teaching in order to fulfill the task of creatively implementing its principles. However, in this "dialogue" way of interacting with the Church's social teaching, a key role is played by the mature faith of those people who need to decide and act in a given place (*in loco*) and time (*in contesto*).

John Paul II:
The truth of salvation illuminates human history

During the Spiritual Exercises of the Roman Curia in March 1976, Cardinal Karol Wojtyla expressed in the presence of Paul VI his own satisfaction with the timely reevaluation of the "world" brought about by *Gaudium et Spes*:

Such a definition of the world was much needed! Not only to form the text of the great Pastoral Constitution, but also to give the key to understanding the signs of the times and, at the same time, the key to the self-awareness of the Church as expressed in the Council, thanks to the acute analysis of all those signs that are put under the common denominator of the concept of contemporaneity: the Church in the contemporary world.[6]

This idea that analyzing the "signs of the times" allows the Church to enter into contact with the contemporary moment will become part of the Magisterium of John Paul II. This means that contemporary history is open to the fulfillment of salvation, and it enriches the Church's understanding of itself.

In the very first words of his first encyclical, *Redemptor Hominis*, history is indicated as the place or locus in which the lordship of Christ is manifested: "The Redeemer of humanity, Jesus Christ, is the center of the universe and of history" (*RH* 1).[7]

However, in the subsequent *Dives in Misericordia,* the pope seems to take pains to tone down an overly enthusiastic view of history. In its very first lines he states:

The situation of the world today not only displays transformations that give grounds for hope in a better future for man on earth, but also reveals a multitude of threats, far surpassing those known up till now. Without ceasing to point out these threats on various occasions (as in addresses at UNO, to UNESCO, to FAO and elsewhere), the Church must at the same time examine them in the light of the truth received from God. (*DiM* 2)

---

[6] K. Wojtyla, *Segno di contraddizione*, Gribaudi, Milano 1977, 54 [our translation]. See *Sign of Contradiction* (New York: Seabury Press, 1979).

[7] Cf. I. Korzeniowski, *I segni dei tempi nel pensiero di Giovanni Paolo II*, EDB, Bologna 1997, 25–43.

In this brief passage, a twofold clarification seems to emerge: first of all, as stated by Paul VI, contemporary history bears a certain ambiguity. The "signs of the times" are not immediately transparent. Therefore, what is seen today as a transformation promising to improve human life could tomorrow constitute a threat. Second, given this ambivalence, the Church must continually examine, undertake its own discernment, in the light of the *truth* revealed by God.

This emphasis on the truth that the Church has received from God, and which therefore always transcends history, appears to be an invitation to redirect the way of theological reflection along the safer path of the deductive method.

This seems to be confirmed by *Laborem Exercens,* in which the pope justifies his option. According to John Paul II, in order to shed light on the reality of human work, the Church must not take the current situation of crisis as its starting point; neither must its examination begin by detecting phenomena such as unemployment or exploitation. Rather, in undertaking its own evaluation, the Church is bound by the need to explain divine Revelation and refer to natural law.

In order to dispel any doubts, the encyclical maintains that the Church should not address humankind by making use of historical analysis, but on the basis of the Word of God:

> The Church is convinced that work is a fundamental dimension of man's existence on earth. She is confirmed in this conviction by considering the whole heritage of the many sciences devoted to man: anthropology, paleontology, history, sociology, psychology, and so on; they all seem to bear witness to this reality in an irrefutable way. But the source of the Church's conviction is above all the revealed word of God, and therefore what is a conviction of the intellect is also a conviction of faith. The reason is that the Church—and it is worthwhile stating it at this point—believes in man: she thinks of man and addresses herself to him not only in the light of historical

experience, not only with the aid of the many methods of scientific knowledge, but in the first place in the light of the revealed word of the living God. Relating herself to man, she seeks to express the eternal designs and transcendent destiny which the living God, the Creator and Redeemer, has linked with him. (*LE* 4)

Similarly in the Apostolic Exhortation *Familiaris Consortio*, John Paul II affirms that "history is not simply a fixed progression toward what is better," since it "presents positive and negative aspects: the first are a sign of the salvation of Christ operating in the world; the second, a sign of the refusal that man gives to the love of God" (*FC* 5). Needing to relativize the tools of the social sciences leads him to affirm that "the Church values sociological and statistical research, when it proves helpful in understanding the historical context." Above all, it is in "following Christ [that] the Church seeks the truth." The conclusion reached in his reasoning confirms that the magisterial function is "normative" for the People of God: "It is the task of the apostolic ministry to ensure that the Church remains in the truth of Christ and to lead her ever more deeply into that truth" (*FC* 6).

In the Encyclical *Sollicitudo Rei Socialis*, addressing the issue of technological and economic development, John Paul II insists on approaching social issues by means of a "correct approach," that is, starting from the doctrinal teaching of the Church. He specifies that only in this way—by adopting a deductive method—is it possible to highlight how human sin lies at the root of social problems.

In today's difficult situation, a more exact awareness and a wider diffusion of the set of principles for reflection, criteria for judgment and directives for action proposed by the Church's teaching would be of great help in promoting both the correct definition of the problems being faced and the best solution to them. It will thus be seen at once that the questions facing us are above all moral questions; and that neither the analysis of the problem of development as such nor the means to overcome the present difficulties can ignore this essential dimension. (*SrS* 41)

Exceptions to this are some texts that run through the Magisterium of this immense pontificate,[8] which stands out for the vastness of the topics that he dealt with in all his official pronouncements.

For example, in *Pastores Dabo Vobis* there is a revival of the inductive method as the instrument with which the Church is called to form priests "who are truly able to respond to the demands of our times." However, John Paul II proposes a reformulation that seems intentionally to offer a specific corrective. On the one hand, he affirms the priority of *knowing* the difficulties present in the historical and cultural context, aware of the problems that seminarians need to live with. On the other hand, he specifies that this activity of knowing must not be reduced to "a simple collection of data." Indeed, knowledge always implies "an interpretative reading" of reality. To examine is already to discern, since the outcome of a reflection is conditioned by the way in which the very elements being investigated are acquired. *Knowing* presupposes an asymmetry in the relationship between theological and scientific data. Otherwise, it is not possible to go beyond what science is able to say. In this way, there is no doubt about the importance of "seeing" reality. Rather, there is an insistence that reality must be "seen" with the eyes of faith. As far as the evaluation of seminarians is concerned, since the current moment is marked by "ambivalence and at times contradiction," and since it presents both "negative elements and reasons for hope" intertwined, in expressing a judgment, account should not be taken only

---

[8] The vast and varied magisterium of John Paul II includes fourteen encyclicals, forty-five apostolic letters, fifteen exhortations, and eleven constitutions, in addition to innumerable addresses and homilies.

of "positive factors," but should "subject the positive factors themselves to careful discernment" (*PdV* 10).

Pope John Paul focused on the act of *knowing*, which analogically corresponds with *reading* the present, and indicates a precise direction. It is not enough to discern between good and evil, one must distinguish between good and better. The inductive method is insufficient if it is not contextualized within the framework of values that tradition has codified through its moral reflection.

Another significant text is found in *Novo Millennio Ineunte*, in which the pope explicitly refers to *Gaudium et Spes* 4 and 44:

> In the common experience of humanity, for all its contradictions, the Spirit of God, who "blows where he wills" (Jn 3:8), not infrequently reveals signs of his presence which help Christ's followers to understand more deeply the message which they bear. Was it not with this humble and trust-filled openness that the Second Vatican Council sought to read "the signs of the times"? Even as she engages in an active and watchful discernment aimed at understanding the "genuine signs of the presence or the purpose of God," the Church acknowledges that she has not only given but has also "received from the history and from the development of the human race." This attitude of openness, combined with careful discernment, was adopted by the Council also in relation to other religions. It is our task to follow with great fidelity the Council's teaching and the path which it has traced. (*NmI* 156)

The use of the expression "the signs of the times" and the celebration of the steps taken by the Church following *Gaudium et Spes*, including in the field of interreligious dialogue, could be seen as circumstantial evidence of John Paul II's desire to deepen the perspective inaugurated by the Second Vatican Council. At the same time, he is firmly convinced of the need to provide a clearer lens through which to examine the Council event itself, in order to reveal its novelty in the light of the teachings already contained in the Tradition of the Church.

Benedict XVI:
The Word of God unveils social evils

John Paul's successor, Benedict XVI, moved in this same direction. From Benedict's point of view, in order to implement a correct "hermeneutic of reform, of renewal in continuity,"[9] it is necessary to deepen the relationship among reason, faith, and history. The theology of the "signs of the times" also needed proper contextualization and had to be supported by a solid theoretical basis firmly rooted in the Tradition of the Church.

This critical framework reflects the same observations made at the Council by the young Joseph Ratzinger, expressing his reservations about the concept of the "signs of the times." He proposed omitting it from the text of *Gaudium et Spes* 4.[10] His intervention lamented its excessive sociological emphasis and the lack of criteria for clarifying its meaning in a biblical-theological key. He also critiqued the absence of an adequate definition of the concept of "world" to which the "signs of the times" refers and an overly naive vision of history that did not highlight the ambivalence of human progress. Above all, he denounced the lack of a *theology of the Cross* that would link the significance of the "signs of the times" to the reality of sin that marks the drama of human history.[11]

---

[9] Pope Benedict XVI, *Address to the Roman Curia Offering Them His Christmas Greetings,* December 22, 2005.

[10] Cf. Joseph A. Komonchak, "Le valutazioni sulla *Gaudium et spes*: Chenu, Dossetti, Ratzinger," in *Volti di fine concilio: Studi di storia e teologia sulla conclusione del Vaticano II,* ed. Joseph Doré and Alberto Melloni (Bologna: Il Mulino, 2000), 115–53.

[11] The German episcopate proposed that the text should become not a constitution but a final encyclical and that, therefore, its message should be less binding. Cf. A. Toniolo, "Vaticano II, pastorale, segni dei tempi: problemi ermeneutici e opportunità ecclesiali," *in Archivio Teologico torinese* XX (2014), 19–34.

In spite of his perplexities, Benedict XVI referred to the "signs of the times" on several occasions during his pontificate, even though its use in his Magisterium tends to oscillate between the sociological and theological domains, and so one cannot arrive at an unequivocal meaning.

For example, in *Caritas in Veritate*, the meaning remains vague and the expression "signs of the times" refers to everything that can constitute a favorable opportunity for the Church to interpret and offer "what she possesses as her characteristic attribute: a global vision of man and of the human race" (*CiV* 18).

In *Verbum Domini*, on the other hand, the category is spelled out in such a way as to resemble the prophetic language of denunciation. A broad meaning remains, whereby the "signs of the times" are taken to include every expression of evil that in social reality gives rise to situations of manipulation and oppression:

> The word of God itself unambiguously denounces injustices and promotes solidarity and equality. In the light of the Lord's words, let us discern the "signs of the times" present in history, and not flee from a commitment to those who suffer and the victims of forms of selfishness. (*VD* 100)

In both cases, however, Benedict XVI is keen to point out that this ability to detect the potentialities and iniquities present in society is developed exclusively on the basis of our relationship with the Word of God.

In another public address, Benedict XVI characterizes the "signs of the times" as including all those manifestations that reflect the restlessness and search for meaning of the human person today. This distinctive trait of contemporary culture can motivate the Church to confirm its own theological discourse, since the quest for meaning encourages an analysis of those reasons for the credibility of faith that allow the Gospel to be proclaimed with effective "realism":

Our way of living in faith and charity becomes a way of speaking of God today, because it shows, through a life lived in Christ, the credibility and realism of what we say with words, which are not solely words but reveal the reality, the true reality. And in this we must take care to perceive the signs of the times in our epoch, namely, to identify the potentials, aspirations, and obstacles we encounter in today's culture and in particular the wish for authenticity, the yearning for transcendence, and concern to safeguard Creation and to communicate fearlessly the response that faith in God offers.[12]

In Chapter 4 of the book-length interview *Light of the World*,[13] the "signs of the times" are identified among the phenomena of degradation that are evident in today's society. They represent so many challenges to the Gospel and the mission of the Church: secularization, the environmental catastrophe, individualism, and the tyranny of relativism. Besides these disastrous results of modernity, there is also the increase in migratory flows as a "sign of the times" of our era:

One of the recognizable *signs of the times* today is undoubtedly migration, a phenomenon which during the century just ended can be said to have taken on structural characteristics, becoming an important factor of the labor market worldwide, a consequence among other things of the enormous drive of globalization. Naturally in this "sign of the times" various factors play a part. They include both national and international migration, forced and voluntary migration, legal and illegal migration, subject also to the scourge of trafficking in human beings.

---

[12] Pope Benedict XVI, *General Audience,* Wednesday, November 28, 2012.

[13] Cf. P. Seewald, *Light of the World: The Pope, the Church, and the Signs of the Times* (San Francisco: Ignatius Press, 2010).

Nor can the category of foreign students, whose numbers increase every year in the world, be forgotten.[14]

In this case, the category "signs of the times" refers to a specific human phenomenon, emphasizing its breadth and complexity. It does not easily lend itself to a precise description, since it involves many diverse facets and dynamics. At first glance, the use of "signs of the times" seems to respond to a purely sociological viewpoint or comprehension. However, Benedict XVI suggests referring it to a further level, that of theological interpretation. Migrations represent a *kairòs* for the Church, because they challenge faith and move believers to question themselves on the right stance to adopt in social relations.

What is striking is the hermeneutical framework in which Benedict XVI inserts the idea of the "signs of the times." He frames the expression as a negative evaluation of the contemporary world. The category thus evokes the multiplicity of social misdeeds that we are witnessing today and urges recovering the reference to the Word of God and the Magisterium of the Church as providing order and clarity for a current situation marked by the chaotic effects of human sin. In doing so, Benedict XVI repeatedly uses the expression "signs of the times" in a way that departs from the original intention of the Council Fathers.

Such a demonization of history lines up in some ways with that apologetic necessity that the Church's social teaching had acknowledged in the pre-conciliar social encyclicals. But this reflects a very different approach from the inductive one proposed in *Octogesima Adveniens*: in order to face the problems of present reality, the faithful will have to turn to the teaching of the Magisterium and adhere to the universal principles illustrated by the social teaching of the Church. In no way should the faithful embark on a solution that does not take these essential references as a starting point, nor should they develop their own

---

[14] Pope Benedict XVI, *"Migrations: A Sign of the Times,"* *Message for the 92nd World Day of Migrants and Refugees,* October 18, 2005.

reflection grounded in faith, on the basis of the circumstances and experiences of a particular community.

In short, the broad semantic spectrum assigned by Benedict XVI to the expression "the signs of the times" actually ends up diluting its effectiveness and relativizing its significant value as a distinctive feature of *Gaudium et Spes*. It almost appears that Benedict blurs the contours of the term in order to avoid defining its precise meaning. His Magisterium seemed to prefer using the category in a mainly sociological sense, directing the interpretation of the Council along other paths and with a view to consolidating the deductive method.

Francis:
The revival of the conciliar perspective of Gaudium et Spes

As already mentioned, in accepting John XXIII's invitation to privilege "pastoral life" in the work of the Council, Vatican II called into question the notion that pastoral life had its sole root or foundation in doctrine.

Fidelity to the truth codified by doctrine is not sufficient for identifying the Church's pastoral form. Rather, a relationship of concern, care, and reciprocity must be established between the truth of the Gospel and the contemporary historical context. In this way, pastoral life is the historical hermeneutic of Christian truth meaning that the relationship between doctrine and pastoral life cannot be thought of as one way. Interpreting the historical situation is also decisive for the doctrinal understanding and elaboration of the content of faith.[15] In proposing a theology of "the signs of the times" in *Gaudium et Spes,* the Council Fathers wanted to make explicit the correlation between these two aspects. At stake was the development of a theology of contemporary history that was not marginal but structurally directed toward the mission of the Church and

---

[15] Cf. S. Lanza, *Convertire Giona. Pastorale come progetto*, Edizioni OCD, Roma 2005, 113–115.

toward determining the practical ways and means in which to embody the proclamation of the Gospel.

Affirming this orientation, Pope Francis avoids reducing the "signs of the times" to purely social indicators, mere phenomena, that do not express a prophetic call or an intrinsic connection with Christian Revelation. In *Evangelii Gaudium* we find a practically programmatic declaration of his way of reading the "signs of the times":

> It is not the task of the pope to offer a detailed and complete analysis of contemporary reality, but I do exhort all the communities to an "ever watchful scrutiny of the signs of the times." This is in fact a grave responsibility, since certain present realities, unless effectively dealt with, are capable of setting off processes of dehumanization which would then be hard to reverse. We need to distinguish clearly what might be a fruit of the kingdom from what runs counter to God's plan. This involves not only recognizing and discerning spirits, but also—and this is decisive—choosing movements of the spirit of good and rejecting those of the spirit of evil. I take for granted the different analyses which other documents of the universal magisterium have offered, as well as those proposed by the regional and national conferences of bishops. In this Exhortation I claim only to consider briefly, and from a pastoral perspective, certain factors which can restrain or weaken the impulse of missionary renewal in the Church, either because they threaten the life and dignity of God's people or because they affect those who are directly involved in the Church's institutions and in her work of evangelization. (*EG* 51)

Traditionally, in the footsteps of his predecessors, Francis notes the ambivalence of the "signs of the times" (*ES* 54; *DiM* 2), as well as the risk of a reductionist approach limited to distinguishing between good and evil (*PdV* 10). At the same time, he declares his intention to address social issues with "a pastoral outlook." His way of proceeding is therefore attentive to the indications of the *Gaudium et Spes* and proceeds inductively, that is, open to receiving contributions from other disciplines with specific competences. Francis affirms that it is not the pope's role to "have a monopoly on the interpretation of social realities or the proposal of solutions to contemporary problems" or to already have at hand the solutions to the problems that now arise (*EG* 184). Rather, avoiding a top-down stance, he humbly asks the Church to listen to the world.

In *Laudato Si'*, Pope Francis also argues that by persisting in a self-referential attitude, in sterile repetitions, theological discourse can only wander down the way of insignificance:

> Theological and philosophical reflections on the situation of humanity and the world can sound tiresome and abstract, unless they are grounded in a fresh analysis of our present situation, which is in many ways unprecedented in the history of humanity. So, before considering how faith brings new incentives and requirements with regard to the world of which we are a part, I will briefly turn to what is happening to our common home. (*LS* 17)

The stakes are high. Repeating a message that does not encounter contemporary history and does not dialogue with today's humanity risks being marginalized. Before risking an evaluation that could turn abstract, Pope Francis suggests considering the facts and coming face to face with the concrete reality of the situation, not in an attempt to "amass information or to satisfy curiosity, but rather to become painfully aware, to dare to turn what is happening to the world into our own personal suffering and thus to discover what each of us can do about it" (*LS* 19). Personal feelings should play a role in this examination and be valued as part of the ecclesial process of evangelical discernment.

In this way, the pope can address everyone, giving his discourse an existential tone that goes beyond adherence to faith. This attitude admits that the Church does not have an exclusive monopoly on the truth. In the case of ecology, for example, Pope Francis begins by describing the current state of the planet and undertakes to look for the causes that have led to this critical situation. He denounces the damaging trend of scientific research centered on the idea of irresponsible progress, the individualism underlying the "throwaway culture" (*LS* 22), and the fragmented vision of the ecological crisis (*LS* 111). Only after establishing common ground on which to base his views does Pope Francis outline the specific contribution that faith can offer in the current crisis (*LS* 62), indicating in the light that shines from the Gospel the origin of that inexhaustible richness that is the faith's own.

This faith-filled view makes it possible to better understand the causes of the ecological crisis and to discern more effectively the direction to be taken to implement an integral ecology. It is by examining problems in this existential key that it is possible to identify useful strategies for taking action.

It is worth pointing out that orientation for action cannot simply be deduced from having "judged" or "evaluated." Moving from reflection to action always needs room for people's creativity and freedom. Whether the orientation is toward action (in the case of thinking inductively) or toward values (thinking deductively), this is a complex interplay of factors that drives significant decisions and subsequent actions.

Among the options for moving forward, Francis points to honest, transparent, and inclusive dialogue. Through dialogue, it is possible to achieve a convergence of views regarding the model of sustainable development to be adopted (*LS* 166), the need to educate generations in how to care (*LS* 230–231), and Christian witness (*LS* 217).

There is something intangible and free that can only emerge from discernment according to the Holy Spirit. After all, even the great scientific discoveries of the modern era did not depend on deductions made at a desk, but on intuitions that went beyond empirical data. If "see-judge-act" is a limited inductive method that thinks it can "scientifically" proceed from social data to pastoral action, by contrast the deductive method, convinced that it can determine how to act starting from universally valid principles, risks being incapable of detecting the complexity of reality.

In science as in pastoral life, however, there is a virtuous cycle to run between theory and practice, since it is not possible to pass unidirectionally from one to the other in a rigorous and convincing way.

At this point, we can conclude that a fact or event becomes a "sign of the times" when it proves capable of permanently changing the mentality and behavior of believers, that is, when it inspires a shared awareness that can modify in a messianic or saving direction the balance of human relations in a given age or period.

3.

CRITERIA FOR DISCERNMENT:
READING THE "SIGNS OF THE TIMES"

Integrating the ecclesiological perspective of Vatican II and following the teaching of *Lumen Gentium*, Pope Francis affirms that "it is precisely the path of synodality which God expects of the Church in the third millennium."[1] At the same time, he argued that synodality "offers us the most adequate interpretative framework for understanding the hierarchical ministry itself." He traces the image of a Church that—like "an inverted pyramid" in which "the top is located beneath the base"[2]—harmonizes all those involved: the People of God, the College of Bishops, and, within it as a bishop among bishops, the successor of Peter.

In *Evangelii Gaudium*, Francis gave a new impetus to the doctrine of the faithful's sense of faith (*sensus fidei fidelium*) (*EG* 119), arguing that the path of synodality is an indispensable prerequisite for infusing the Church with a renewed missionary thrust: all members of the Church are active subjects of evangelization and "missionary disciples" (*EG* 120).

Lay people represent the vast majority of the People of God, and there is much to learn from their participation in the various expressions of the life and mission of ecclesial

---

[1] Pope Francis, *Address at the Commemoration of the 50th Anniversary of the Synod of Bishops*, October 17, 2015.

[2] Ibid.

communities: from their devotion expressed in popular piety, from their involvement in ordinary pastoral life, and from their specific competence in the various areas of cultural and social life (*EG* 126).

It is therefore necessary to overcome the obstacles posed by the lack of formation and of recognized spaces in which the lay faithful can express themselves and take an active part, as well as by a clerical mentality that risks keeping the lay people on the margins of ecclesial life (*EG* 102).

The co-responsibility of the entire People of God for the mission of the Church also requires launching processes of consultation that make the presence and voice of lay people more participatory. This is not a question of giving rise to a sort of "lay parliamentarianism," since the authority of the College of Bishops does not depend on a majority vote of the faithful. Rather, the co-responsibility and participation of the laity represent a valuable charism—meant to build up the body and to care for the unity—with which the Spirit has endowed the body of the Church.

In this perspective, the Apostolic Constitution on the Synod of Bishops of September 18, 2018, *Episcopalis Communio*, rendered normative the various steps on the way of a Church that is "constitutively" synodal. Every synodal process "begins by listening to the People of God," "continues by listening to the pastors," and culminates in listening to the Bishop of Rome, called to speak as "pastor and teacher of all Christians."[3]

"The Synod of Bishops," writes Pope Francis in *Episcopalis Communio*, "must increasingly become a privileged instrument for *listening* to the People of God" (*EC* 6). And "although structurally it is essentially configured as an episcopal body, this does not mean that the Synod exists separately from the rest of the faithful. On the contrary, it is a suitable instrument for giving voice to the entire People of God" (*EC* 6). For this reason it is "of great importance" in the preparation of synods

---

[3] Ibid.

"that consultation of all the particular Churches be given special attention" (*EC* 7).

The fundamental question that the path of synodality poses in the life of the Church is a renewed understanding of communion understood in terms of inclusiveness: to involve all the components of the People of God, under the authority of those whom the Holy Spirit establishes as pastors of the Church, in such a way that everyone may feel co-responsible in the life and mission of the Church.

We conclude this first part of the book by drawing out five criteria that Francis indicates to encourage the worldwide Church and "each particular Church to undertake a resolute process of discernment, purification and reform" (*EG* 30). These are five principles oriented toward synodality, so that all the baptized can acquire and interiorize a spirituality that is not individualist but open to communion. Without a real conversion in our way of thinking and acting, without constantly striving to grow in mutual acceptance, the external means of communion—the ecclesial structures put in place by the Council—can prove insufficient in achieving the end for which they were created.[4]

First criterion:
Faith that discerns "lifestyles"

At the Synod of Bishops in 2012, the Synod Fathers chose to address the urgent issue of the new evangelization. Paying particular attention to the growing phenomenon of secularization in the West, they emphasized that the commitment to proclaim the Gospel required a careful examination of history and of culture.

Echoing the requests expressed by Vatican II in *Gaudium et Spes*, the Synod reaffirmed that the transmission of the faith always requires careful consideration of the circular relationship between the believing community and the world. To

---

[4] For an application of the five criteria for discernment, see the appendix "After the Pandemic, Siblings All," herein.

orient evangelization to pastoral life, the task of discerning the "signs of the times" becomes a priority, enabling us to decipher "new sectors which have emerged in human history in the last decade, so that, in turn, they might be turned into places for proclaiming the Gospel and experiencing the Church."[5]

If discerning the "signs of the times" is established as an intrinsic and necessary requirement of evangelization, then we must ask what the criteria are for profoundly reading the events around us.

As mentioned above, *Gaudium et Spes* 11 indicates the criterion of *faith*, not understood in purely individualistic terms, but as an expression of the lived experience of the People of God. This affirmation resonates with *Dei Verbum* 8, in which a very broad concept of handing on the faith (*Traditio fidei*) is made explicit. Faith arises from newly understanding the event of Revelation as God's self-communication to humankind. Faith is thus described as a creative dynamism, as a living reality that can progress in time,[6] and following upon the generative relationship between the Gospel and people's contemporary history.

Pope Francis concretely applies the criterion of faith to reading the present when he exhorts everyone to discern "lifestyles," since there is an intimate relationship between the way that people live their lives and what establishes their horizon of meaning. Francis's interpretation of faith in an existential key is an invitation to newly understand the human person as a being who is intrinsically open to relationship with God, with others, with creation, and with oneself (*LS* 104–110; 115; 122).

In this sense, Francis's Magisterium draws on the affirmations with which his predecessors had already recalled this

---

[5] Synod of Bishops, Third Ordinary General Assembly, *The New Evangelization for the Transmission of the Christian Faith: Instrumentum Laboris*, 51.

[6] *DV* 8 uses the verb *proficit* precisely to indicate a development that is enriched over time.

interconnection between style of life and the meaning of life. We can recall, for example, John Paul II's insistence on the need to counteract the systematic alienation that the technological paradigm has introduced into the fabric of human relationships, as well as Benedict XVI's invitation to shed new light on human reason in a broader framework, that is, to reconsider its potentialities within the context of the broader wisdom of the divine *Logos*.

Following his predecessors, Francis denounces how technology risks following a *one-dimensional* model every time that it violates the fundamental relational structure of the human being (*EG* 115).[7] The criterion of faith leads us, then, to distinguish between a "lifestyle according to the Gospel" (*EG* 168) and "a lifestyle that excludes others" (*EG* 67). Faith motivates those who are "slaves of an individualistic mentality" to choose "a lifestyle and way of thinking that is more human, more noble, more fruitful, that gives dignity to their passage on this earth" (*EG* 208).

The encyclical *Laudato Si'* takes up this same distinction in an even more radical way. It contrasts "a consumerist lifestyle" (*LS* 204), in which "various forms of collective selfishness" are reflected, with "a new lifestyle" (*LS* 16) that goes against the trend of the dominant culture.

Ultimately, "the human root of the ecological crisis" is to be found in a certain use of technology that reflects this individualistic style (*LS* 106). Francis points out the irresponsible choices that politics has made in allowing itself to be enslaved to the interests of technology and of finance (*LS* 109). In doing so, Francis refers to the teaching of Pius XI's encyclical *Quadragesimo Anno*, which already in 1931 warned against the drifts of an "individualistic economic science" (*QAn* 89) and "a despotic mastery of the economy in the hands of the few" (*QAn* 105).

---

[7] This point recalls what John XXIII wrote in the encyclical *Mater et Magistra*: "The progress of science and technology in every aspect of life has led, particularly today, to increased relationships between nations, and made the nations more and more dependent on one another" (*MM* 200).

Second criterion:
The common good prevails over the logic of private interest

In distinguishing among various lifestyles, we can understand how Francis's Magisterium appears to show greater attention to the "communal pole" with respect to the "individual interests." This content is not new in the Church's social teaching, but rather a specific concern for the way of rereading the Church's traditional teaching on social doctrine.

In fact, the social teaching of the Church has always affirmed that businesses are aimed at the common good, since all the earth's goods are a gift from God to humanity.[8] The universal destination of goods does not contradict, or even deny, the principle of private property, which the Church's social teaching has also recognized as legitimate. But it does point out the non-absolute character of private property, defining its limits (*LS* 93).

In this regard, in *Sollicitudo Rei Socialis* John Paul II speaks of a "social mortgage" on private property:

> It is necessary to state once more the characteristic principle of Christian social doctrine: the goods of this world are originally meant for all. The right to private property is valid and necessary, but it does not nullify the value of this principle. Private property, in fact, is under a "social mortgage," which means that it has an intrinsically

---

[8] In *Gaudium et Spes*, the Council defined the "common good" as "the sum of those conditions of social life which allow social groups and their individual members relatively thorough and ready access to their own fulfillment" (*GS* 26). The *Compendium* on the Church's social teaching specifies: "The common good does not consist in the simple sum of the particular goods of each subject of a social entity. Belonging to everyone and to each person, it is and remains "common," because it is indivisible and because only together is it possible to attain it, increase it and safeguard its effectiveness, with regard also to the future" (Pontifical Council for Justice and Peace, *Compendium of the Social Doctrine of the Church*, 164).

social function, based upon and justified precisely by the principle of the universal destination of goods. (*SrS* 42)

In *Laudato Si'*, Francis explicitly refers to the statements of his predecessor, affirming that the right to private property is not unconditional:

The Christian tradition has never recognized the right to private property as absolute or inviolable, and has stressed the social purpose of all forms of private property. Saint John Paul II forcefully reaffirmed this teaching, stating that "God gave the earth to the whole human race for the sustenance of all its members, without excluding or favoring anyone." These are strong words. He noted that "a type of development which did not respect and promote human rights—personal and social, economic, and political, including the rights of nations and of peoples—would not be really worthy of man." He clearly explained that "the Church does indeed defend the legitimate right to private property, but she also teaches no less clearly that there is always a social mortgage on all private property, in order that goods may serve the general purpose that God gave them." Consequently, he maintained, "it is not in accord with God's plan that this gift be used in such a way that its benefits favor only a few." This calls into serious question the unjust habits of a part of humanity. (*LS* 93)

What is distinctive in Francis's approach to the issue of private property is how he takes on the viewpoint of the last and the least, placing himself on the side of the poor (*ex parte pauperum*), and not vice versa. This has him speak out against a reductionist approach to the economy that is based on the idea that the social responsibility of those who own companies is to maximize profit, to the point of legitimizing an instrumental use of the environment and of people, even at the cost of rendering them subservient to the financial objective of increasing capital.

For Francis, this "misunderstanding of the very concept of the economy" (*LS* 195) takes into account the interests of only a part of the stakeholders and does not consider "the real value of things, their significance for people and cultures, or the concerns and needs of the poor" (*LS* 190). However, highlighting the social responsibilities of companies in a framework that takes seriously the welfare of all does not mean denying companies the right to pay a fair return to the shareholders involved, given the risks they take with their investments.[9]

Businesses can create capital not only by taking the path of *competition*, which often ends up trampling on the rights of the earth and the poor, but by choosing the path of *cooperation* and *solidarity*. In this sense, *Laudato Si'* recalls the teaching on "social capital" (*LS* 128) that Benedict XVI amply developed in *Caritas in Veritate*:

> The Church's social doctrine holds that authentically human social relationships of friendship, solidarity, and reciprocity can also be conducted within economic activity, and not only outside it or "after" it. The economic sphere is neither ethically neutral, nor inherently inhuman and opposed to society. It is part and parcel of human activity and precisely because it is human, it must be structured and governed in an ethical manner. The great challenge before us, accentuated by the problems of development in this global era and made even more urgent by the economic and financial crisis, is to demonstrate, in thinking and behavior, not only that traditional principles of social ethics like transparency, honesty, and responsibility cannot be ignored or attenuated, but also that in commercial relationships the principle of gratuitousness and the logic

---

[9] In pointing out, however, that profit should not be the main aim of businesses, but that other aspects should also be taken into account, Francis is in continuity with *Centesimus Annus*, which states: "Profit is a regulator of the life of a business, but it is not the only one; *other human and moral factors* must also be considered which, in the long term, are at least equally important for the life of a business" (*CA* 35).

of gift as an expression of fraternity can and must find their place within normal economic activity. (*CiV* 36)

Pope Francis can thus claim that solidarity is as much a moral as an economic imperative.[10] Profit will be ethical only when the economic and social costs arising from the use of environmental resources by those who benefit from them do not harm other populations or mortgage the future of generations to come (*LS* 195).

The principle of solidarity has companies consider their social responsibilities, evaluating the impact of their choices on other variables and not only the parameter of market value. Consequently, the implementation of subsidiarity will also imply respect for the dignity of the person and a firm resolve to contribute to the promotion of personal initiative, so that everyone may personally benefit from the conditions necessary for the development of his or her skills. Subsidiarity manifests itself as "a spirit of generous care" (*LS* 220) and aims to enhance personal qualities and the "willingness to learn from one another" (*LS* 214).

Third criterion:
The realism of effective charity

John Paul II recalls how the Church's social teaching represents not a middle way between libertarian capitalism and Marxist collectivism but which is rooted in and constantly referring to the Word of God, an entirely different option. Not an ideology, Catholic social teaching applies Gospel principles to human life in person and in society (*SrS* 41).

Benedict XVI completes the meaning of these affirmations by deepening the relationship between the Gospel and works: this social teaching is proclamation of the truth of Christ's love

---

[10] Cf. W. D. Montgomery, "The Flawed Economics of *Laudato Si'*," *New Atlantis* 47 (2015): 31–44.

in society, charity in truth in social matters, *caritas in veritate in re sociali* (*CiV* 5) in the sense that Christians express their identity by being a "subject of charity." Benedict tells us that baptized persons can order their life toward witness by disposing themselves to the love of God and hungering for this love as the true substance of every other relationship—both interpersonally and socially. Through works of charity, baptized persons make visible the truth of what they have become, thanks to the gift of Christ.

The orientation of the social teaching of the Church, as outlined in the Magisterium of John Paul II and Benedict XVI, envisages a substantial, constant, and urgent integration of charity into the typical dynamics of justice, both as the fruit of a more mature reflection and awareness of God's call to love, and as a remedy to the many acts of injustice that disfigure the face of creation and of humanity.[11]

The Magisterium of Francis develops all the implications of this focus of his predecessors to underline the link between social commitment and evangelical charity. In particular, Francis acknowledges Benedict XVI's call to the concreteness of charity as a way of rendering the proclamation of the Gospel credible.

Indeed, in *Deus Caritas Est* Pope Benedict highlights how faith is not an abstract idea, but an experience that fully involves all the dimensions of the human person and that "unites our intellect, will, and sentiments in the all-embracing act of love" (*DCE* 17).

For Francis, living in service to charity, embracing the concreteness of love, means personally encountering the poor, entering into contact with their "flesh," giving love "a body"; it means meeting the "bodies" of our weaker siblings. Following the disconcerting logic of the Incarnation of the Word, the Church is called to have a preferential option for the poor (*EG*

---

[11] As John Paul II noted, love normally expresses itself, in an ethical sense, through the category of "solidarity," since it moves toward overcoming itself and, in the light of faith, tends to take on the specifically Christian dimensions of total gratuity, forgiveness, and reconciliation (*SrS* 40).

48), and to see in this preference the fundamental prerogative of serving charity.[12] The pope points out that this is not simply a sociological preference, but eminently theological, because it connects with the saving action of God throughout the course of salvation history: "Without the preferential option for the poor, the proclamation of the Gospel, which is itself the prime form of charity, risks being misunderstood or submerged by the ocean of words which daily engulfs us in today's society of mass communications" (*EG* 199).

The kenotic or self-emptying orientation that God imposed upon love is a fact; indeed, it is *the* fact, the very revelation of God's face. This way inseparably links faith in God with the willing decision to take on every form of human frailty, every personal and collective experience and expression of poverty. When we speak of charity, then, we must not have a generic image of the poor in mind or an abstract idea of poverty, but rather be referring to someone in "flesh and bone."

It is this "incarnated charitable" service that leads to the *realism of faith* and shows the social dimension of the Gospel. With physical presence, with pain, with needs, but also with joy, the other challenges our faith, anchors it in reality, and leads it to awe and wonder. The Church "abounds in effective charity and a compassion which understands, assists and promotes" (*EG* 179).

Fourth criterion:
The preferential option for the poor

For Francis, the preferential option for the poor is no expression of naive "do-goodism." It means pursuing the process of ecclesial transformation desired and initiated by Vatican II. The Council Fathers, in fact, saw in the least and the weakest of contemporary history a "sign of the times." They were convinced that the Church was called to move from practices

---

[12] Cf. J. Planellas Barnosell, *La Iglesia de los pobres en el Concilio Vaticano II*, Herder, Barcelona 2014.

of charity in which the poor are reduced to a mere "object" of care, to recognizing one another as "subject" and as "member" of the People of God.

The words of Francis, therefore, simply bring us back to Vatican II's becoming aware of the need to privilege the poor as a call of the Holy Spirit to conversion, a call to convert the internal structures of the Church as well as how we relate to the Gospel. Some texts can be cited as evidence of this continuity:

> Christ was sent by the Father "to bring good news to the poor, to heal the contrite of heart" (Lk 4:18), "to seek and to save what was lost" (Lk 19:10). Similarly, the Church encompasses with love all who are afflicted with human suffering and in the poor and afflicted sees the image of its poor and suffering Founder. It does all it can to relieve their need and in them it strives to serve Christ. (*LG* 8)

Really meaningful are also the words with which the prologue of *Gaudium et Spes* leads us powerfully in this direction, looking "especially" at the poor as the Church's key reference in its desire to engage with the contemporary world:

> The joys and the hopes, the griefs and the anxieties of the men of this age, especially those who are poor or in any way afflicted, these are the joys and hopes, the griefs and anxieties of the followers of Christ. Indeed, nothing genuinely human fails to raise an echo in their hearts. (*GS* 1)

In the same vein, Paul VI's Apostolic Exhortation *Evangelii Nuntiandi* reaffirms that the Church's mission is primarily to proclaim the good news to the poor:

> Going from town to town, preaching to the poorest—who are frequently the most receptive—the joyful news of the fulfillment of the promises and of the Covenant offered by God is the mission for which Jesus declares that He is sent by the Father. (*EN* 6)

For Francis, giving the poor a privileged place among the members of the People of God (*EG* 187–196) means recognizing them not only as privileged recipients of evangelization but also as actors in evangelization. All the baptized are in fact encouraged to consider encountering the poor as a privileged opportunity for letting themselves be evangelized by Christ, for recognizing Christ's presence in them (*EG* 121; 178), and for seizing the opportunity to initiate fruitful exchanges humanly and as believers.

In *Lumen Gentium*, the Council expressed the concept of *catholicity* based on two principles. First is the theological principle, according to which God summons humanity. The second principle is anthropological, according to which everyone is "called to be part of the People of God" (*LG* 13). Francis translates this teaching of Vatican II into ethical terms by way of the double prism of right and duty. All people have the right to receive the Gospel. All Christians have the duty to proclaim it without excluding anyone (*EG* 14). Francis's insistence on the need to return to the self-emptying *kerygma*—the core message of the Gospel—seems to overcome the distinction between the hierarchy who teach and the laity who listen, since everyone is involved in the Church's mission of proclaiming the Gospel; and between evangelizers and evangelized, because even among the baptized there are many who have not received the Gospel. Francis arrives at the conclusion that "we must all let others evangelize us constantly" (*EG* 121; 174).

The four criteria of discernment (*EG* 222–237) offered by Francis lay out the idea of catholicity as a reality in tension, in which opposing poles underline the Church's dynamic call to integrate everyone in its mission of seeking the truth: space-time, unity-conflict, reality-idea, whole-part. Evangelization, therefore, must not be understood as an activity that primarily rests with the individual, but as a mission that concerns the Church in its entirety. The subject of the mission is the whole People of God, and this calls for every pastoral initiative to be situated "in a broader growth process and the integration of every dimension of the person within a communal journey of hearing and response" (*EG* 166). The poor are also evangelizers, because as members of the People of God they have much to give and much to teach, and for this reason they must never be abandoned (*EG* 48).

Incorporating the teaching of Saint John Paul II, poverty is described not only in material terms as indigence, but extends to every form of the person's impoverishment, every limitation or injury to the dignity and fundamental rights of the human being (*SrS* 15).

Since his election as the Bishop of Rome, Pope Francis has urged believers to start from the peripheries—not only the geographical but also the existential ones—following the invitation of the Lord, who knocks from inside the doors of our hearts and asks to go out to encounter people.

In this light, it becomes clear why it is necessary to "put all things in a missionary key" (*EG* 34). Being attentive to social justice and to the personal stories of those in desperate conditions—experiences of pain, poverty, and misery—translates into the active task of decentralizing the Church and adopting a new, forward-looking pastoral vision (*EG* 30). The development of a multifaceted or polyhedral model of ecclesial and social unity (*EG* 234–237) thus reflects a renewed ecumenical and interreligious sensitivity and allows us to pursue a different economic and environmental approach.

The real challenge for the Church of our time is responding to people who "thirst for God" (*EG* 89; 165). The question to be addressed is no longer that of atheism, as it was for *Gaudium et Spes*, which declared it to be an unoriginal phenomenon (*GS* 19), but shifts to what is proper (*proprium*) or essential to human beings. It is no longer a question of how to talk about God to the non-believer, but how to mediate God to those living in subhuman conditions. Here the center of gravity shifts from Western culture to the peripheries of the world, where the problem for millions of people consists in living an inhuman existence. How to announce to them that God is Father?

The anthropology of Francis is a total Christian anthropology. It follows the direction outlined by Paul VI regarding the true development of "every man and the whole man" (*PP* 14; *EG* 181). This restores an image of the human as an emerging subject, as creatures called to become persons and to achieve their own identity. Western culture, imbued with religious indifference, does not make it easy to achieve this objective and needs to pay attention to building up personal identity, without which it is not possible to share in Christian experience. For this reason, the pope urges pastors and lay Christians to "accompany with mercy and patience the eventual stages of personal growth as these progressively occur" (*EG* 44).

Fifth criterion:
Care for creation

When Francis calls "every Christian" (*EG* 3) and "every person" (*LS* 3) to his or her responsibility,[13] especially in showing "concern for the vulnerable" (*EG* 209–216), he turns his attention not only to the *poor*, but also to the *earth*.

From his perspective, becoming attentive to the "cry of the poor" puts us in a position to listen to the cry of our sister the earth, who "cries out to us because of the harm we have inflicted on her by our irresponsible use and abuse of the goods with which God has endowed her" (*LS* 2). Francis insists on the intimate relationship between care for the environment and care for the poor:

> Today, however, we have to realize that a true ecological approach always becomes a social approach; it must integrate questions of justice in debates on the environment, so as to hear both the cry of the earth and the cry of the poor. (*LS* 49)

---

[13] The choice of addressing everyone stands in continuity with the approach of the Second Vatican Council, which declared that it "addresses itself without hesitation, not only to the sons of the Church and to all who invoke the name of Christ, but to the whole of humanity" (*GS* 2).

Francis insists on this point with even greater clarity in the post-synodal apostolic exhortation *Querida Amazonia*:

> If God calls us to listen both to the cry of the poor and that of the earth, then for us, the cry of the Amazon region to the Creator is similar to the cry of God's people in Egypt (cf. Ex 3:7). It is a cry of slavery and abandonment pleading for freedom. (*QA* 52)

The connection between the poor and the environment makes it possible to focus on how the future of all of humanity is intimately linked to that of the environment, so that protecting the interests of the weaker very often coincides with safeguarding creation. This means, first and foremost, paying attention to the unheard voices of the excluded, of all those who—despite being mentioned in international political and economic debates—remain unheard. Their problems "are brought up as an afterthought, a question which gets added almost out of duty or in a tangential way, if not treated merely as collateral damage" (*LS* 49).

By focusing on those sectors of the population that are most exposed to climate change, Francis takes a stand against an anthropocentric interpretation—considered by many as being of Christian origin[14]—that has often ended up legitimizing the irresponsible exploitation of environmental resources and showing various forms of disdain toward the other living beings that populate the earth. The problem, then, shifts once again to the understanding of the human person and the way we understand our central role in creation.[15]

---

[14] The Catholic Church was accused by leading scientists of being directly responsible for the ecological crisis as a result of its anthropological vision. Cf. L. White, "The Historical Roots of Our Ecological Crisis," *Science* 3767 (1967): 1203–1207.

[15] Cf. B. Sajaloli and É. Gresillon, "L'Église catholique et l'anthropocène," *Nouvelles perspectives en sciences sociales* 14, no. 2 (2019): 109–152.

Evangelii Gaudium also sets out four principles that offer a starting point for addressing the question of the common good and social peace. We briefly mention them here:

- Time is greater than space;
- Unity prevails over conflict;
- Reality is more important than ideas;
- The whole is greater than the part. (*EG* 222–237)

It is the third principle that takes on particular significance when Francis explains that the "myth of progress" (*LS* 60; 78) drives the omnipresent technocratic paradigm. The ideology underlying techno-scientific progress is nourished by an anthropocentric perspective that the pope tries to contextualize and redefine in the light of recent historical developments and the declarations of Vatican II.

While we read in *Gaudium et Spes* that "all things on earth should be related to man as their center and crown" (*GS* 12), Francis denounces the excesses deriving from a "distorted" or "despotic anthropocentrism" (*LS* 69; 118–119; 122), stating instead that "the earth is essentially a shared inheritance whose fruits are meant to benefit everyone" (*LS* 93).

The earth is a good that human beings must share with all living things. In benefiting from it, we must consider not only our own benefit, but the good of all.[16] Benedict XVI was on the same wavelength in his encyclical *Caritas in Veritate*, in which he highlighted the interconnection between social life and the environment:

The way humanity treats the environment influences the way it treats itself, and vice versa. This invites contemporary society to a serious review of its lifestyle, which, in many parts of the world, is prone to hedonism and

---

[16] Cf. L. A. Silecchia, "Conflicts and *Laudato Si'*: Ten Principles for Environmental Dispute Resolution," *Journal of Land Use and Environmental Law* 33, no. 1 (2017): 61–86.

consumerism, regardless of their harmful consequences. What is needed is an effective shift in mentality which can lead to the adoption of new lifestyles "in which the quest for truth, beauty, goodness, and communion with others for the sake of common growth are the factors which determine consumer choices, savings and investments." Every violation of solidarity and civic friendship harms the environment, just as environmental deterioration in turn upsets relations in society. Nature, especially in our time, is so integrated into the dynamics of society and culture that by now it hardly constitutes an independent variable. (*CiV* 51)

Being grounded in reality against every idealism and mystification means avoiding the extremes of both anthropocentrism and biocentrism (*LS* 118), in order to aim for what Paul VI called a "full-bodied humanism" (*PP* 42). The legitimate autonomy of earthly realities (*GS* 36) is thus recalled and clarified within the framework of a more mature and balanced theology of creation (*LS* 80; 99).

The socio-environmental sphere struggles to overcome the ills of an economic-financial system that generates global inequalities. What is needed instead is to build a sustainable future based on integral ecology. We can realistically assert that peace is possible, if we rediscover the planetary dimension of our existence.[17]

Francis calls human involvement in the environment a form of ministry. He thus takes up the Magisterium of Paul VI, who deserves credit for having observed the relationship between humans and creation from a different perspective. He interpreted the "lordship or sovereignty" exercised by human beings as an expression of service and care. This shift was made possible by interpreting Scripture in a new light, whereby

---

[17] Cf. M. Cremers, "Corporate Social Responsibility in the Light of *Laudato Si'*," *Journal of Corporate Citizenship* 64 (2016): 62–78; cf. P. Escorsa, "La economia del papa Francisco," *El Ciervo* 62, no. 745 (2014): 28–29.

the divine command *"subicite eam"* in Genesis 1:28 (often translated as "subdue the earth") was not divine permission to suppress or exploit creation, but a call to steward and protect God's handiwork.[18]

It was only with John Paul II, however, that an effective inclusion of ecological issues in the theological reflection of the Church began to take place. Over the course of the 1980s and 1990s, the Church's position on the environment was reshaped through exchanges with scientists and ecumenical dialogue. The fundamental link between God and nature became more and more apparent, while at the same time avoiding any kind of pantheism.

The text of *Centesimus Annus* can be read as a culmination of the interchange that began with the Lutheran churches and the Orthodox Church during the meetings of the Ecumenical Council of Churches held between 1990 and 1995:

> Man, who discovers his capacity to transform and in a certain sense create the world through his own work, forgets that this is always based on God's prior and original gift of the things that are. Man thinks that he can make arbitrary use of the earth, subjecting it without restraint to his will, as though it did not have its own requisites and a prior God-given purpose, which man can indeed develop but must not betray. Instead of carrying out his role as a co-operator with God in the work of creation, man sets himself up in place of God and thus ends up provoking a rebellion on the part of nature, which is more tyrannized than governed by him. (*CA* 37)

What is specific about John Paul II's approach to environmental questions is that he perceives them through the lens of defending human life. He develops a "human ecology" in which the right relationship of humankind to the environment is a

---

[18] Cf. T. Rossi, "'La *Laudato Si*' elementi per un'ermeneutica del pensiero di papa Francesco," *Angelicum* 93, no. 1 (2016): 157–190.

consequence of respect for "the natural and moral structure with which he has been endowed" (*CA* 38). Damaging nature is a sin, turning us away from God and weighing on our conscience. In this way, John Paul II refocuses environmental issues on the human person, but from an eminently ethical perspective.

From the proclamation of Saint Francis of Assisi as the patron saint of ecologists in 1979, to the *Joint Declaration* with the Ecumenical Patriarch Bartholomew I in 2002, the magisterium of John Paul II marked a true ecological conversion. In the text of *Ecclesia in Europa*, he put forth a path for the Church's action for generations to come:

> Finally, it cannot be forgotten that at times improper use is made of the goods of the earth. By failing in his mission of cultivating and caring for the land with wisdom and love (cf. Gen 2:15), man has in fact devastated woodlands and plains in many regions, polluted bodies of water, made the air unbreathable, upset hydro-geological and atmospheric systems and caused the desertification of vast areas. In this case too, rendering service to the Gospel of hope means committing ourselves in new ways to a proper use of the goods of the earth, encouraging that sense of concern which, in addition to safeguarding natural habitats, defends the quality of the life of individuals and thus prepares for future generations an environment more in harmony with the Creator's plan. (*EiE* 89)

Likewise in *Caritas in Veritate*, following in his predecessor's footsteps, Benedict XVI maintains that the right relationship between humanity and the environment be measured by morality. "Human beings interpret and shape the natural environment through culture, which in turn is given direction by the responsible use of freedom, in accordance with the dictates of the moral law" (*CiV* 48). Protecting nature is a direct consequence of consistently applying the moral laws to which Christians are called.

From the "human ecology" of John Paul II to the "integral ecology" of Pope Francis, however, there is another turning point—a further step on the path of conversion. *Laudato Si'* points out that "self-improvement on the part of individuals will not by itself remedy the extremely complex situation facing our world today" (*LS* 219). Rather, it is necessary to address social problems by building a network that involves a "community conversion" (*LS* 219).

Unlike John Paul II, who recalled the need for a path of awareness linked to individual choices, Francis calls for a change involving the Church and society as a whole, with decisions that give new direction to people's lifestyles.[19]

Francis calls for a necessary methodological change. The vantage point from which to rethink the relationship with the environment is not the individual, in a necessary moral commitment and consistency, but rather the world's six or seven billion people who are given no voice.

The moral law does not remain in the background but is approached from a different angle that avoids reducing it to subjective choice. In order to face the environmental crisis, scientific competence is not enough, nor is a naive personal willingness to do good. Rather, a common foundation is needed, which Francis calls "a genuine and profound humanism to serve as the basis of a noble and generous society" (*LS* 181; 5).

---

[19] Cf. A. Pelayo, "*Laudato Si',* mucho más que medio ambiente," *Política Exterior* 29, no. 166 (2015): 86–92.

PART II

SIBLINGS ALL AND SOCIAL FRIENDSHIP: A "SIGN OF THE TIMES"

4.

REFLECTING ON THE PROBLEMS, ANALYZING THE CAUSES

(*Fratelli Tutti,* ch. 1)

The proposals launched by the encyclical *Fratelli Tutti* can be appreciated in light of Pope Francis's actions, mentioned in the Introduction of this book, and also of his firm decision to follow up on and implement the teaching of the Second Vatican Council: our all being siblings and social friendship constitute a key "sign of the times" for the world today (*GS* 4).

We have also mentioned that *Gaudium et Spes* outlines the exercise of evangelical discernment, as the faithful's sense of the faith (*sensus fidei fidelium*), in three movements: *scrutinizing* the signs of the times; *interpreting* them in the light of the Gospel; and *responding* to questions of meaning (*GS* 4). No longer dismayed by modernity, Vatican II's *Pastoral Constitution* sets out a reading of today's reality that recognizes the capacity of the human family to shape the world through its own activity. This conviction is grounded in the recognition of the dignity of the human person, seen not as an individual, but as the center and origin of society. This sequence—person, society, human activity—enhances the autonomy of created realities and gives centrality to people's action. The positive elements that emerge from the variety and richness of cultures, from research and the progress of scientific disciplines, and from the efforts and industriousness of human ingenuity, all contribute to manifesting God's saving will for humanity. All this leads us to the following conclusion: "Since the Church has a visible and social structure as a sign of her unity in Christ, she can and ought to be enriched by the development of human social life" (*GS* 44).

In *Fratelli Tutti* we can recognize the trajectory outlined by *Gaudium et Spes*, above all willingly "to hear, distinguish, and interpret the many voices of our age," but also to recognize human social life as the "place" where the Church can "understand it[self] more penetratingly" in the "constitution given her by Christ" and so engage to "express it better, and adjust it more successfully to our times" (*GS* 44).

In the second part of this book, we endeavor to highlight how *Fratelli Tutti* has taken up the inductive method proposed in *Gaudium et Spes*. *Fratelli Tutti*'s structure and way of treating the themes it addresses fully reflect the intention to "scrutinize, interpret, and respond" (cf. *GS* 4). The introductory section of the encyclical (ch. 1) is a careful analysis of the problems that current events pose to humanity as a challenge and an obstacle to our all being siblings and enjoying social friendship. The encyclical then investigates our present time in the light of the Word of God (ch. 2), and discerns the good that today bears as a promise of change and openness to the dynamism of grace (chs. 3–4). Then the path and the means with which to act toward building a better and open world are identified (chs. 5–7). Finally, as if to complete the reflection, the themes already dealt with converge in the appeal which the Pope addresses to Christians and to the other religions to work together responsibly for the peace and unity of the human family (ch. 8).

Siblings all as a "sign of the times"

In the Council's teaching, the "signs of the times" constitute a challenge and a stimulus for "a deeper and more accurate understanding of the faith" (*GS* 62). This affirmation acquires value and significance when read in the light of what *Dei Verbum* establishes regarding "sacred Tradition" (*DV* 10). The Tradition of the Church is no longer presented as a collection of enigmatic doctrines handed down orally by the Apostles and codified once and for all in a rigidly fixed corpus. Rather, it is understood as a dynamic reality, subject to continuous development. Springing from the Easter witness and having its own foundation in the "deposit" (*depositum*) of the apostolic faith in the Risen Lord, it has often been condensed in the course of the Church's history also—but not only—into a "doctrinal corpus."

It is the great merit of Vatican II to have recovered a broader understanding of Tradition, no longer limited to what is contained "in the unwritten traditions received by the Apostles from the very mouth of Christ"[1] and handed down verbally by them, but also understood in reference to the faith uninterruptedly by the Church.

The approach the Council's reflection chooses to adopt in approaching the question of Tradition—which, together with Sacred Scripture, constitutes "one sacred deposit of the Word of God" (*DV* 10)—emphasizes how, in addition to doctrine, Tradition must be traced back to the life and liturgy of the Church, since it consists in a process of global transmission to the generations of every age of "all that she herself is, all that she believes" (*DV* 8).

After reaffirming, in continuity with *Dei Filius*, that divine Revelation does indeed unfold across history, Vatican II emphasizes the intrinsically historical quality of the Church's "real" Tradition.[2] The point here is to emphasize the *dynamic* character of the transmission of the Gospel, which enables us to progress in our understanding of Tradition (*DV* 8).

---

[1] Vatican Council I, Dogmatic Constitution *Dei Filius*, in *Tutte le Encicliche e i principali documenti pontifici emanati dal 1740*, vol. IV: *Pio IX* (1846–1878), ed. U. Bellocchi, Libreria Editrice Vaticana, Città del Vaticano 1995, 321—our translation.

[2] Cf. S. Pié-Ninot, *La Teología Fundamental*, Secr. Trinitario, Salamanca 2009, 593–595.

Tradition, understood as the communication of the living substance of the Gospel, does not take place by virtue of theological deductions, but rather through the participation of all the members of the People of God and by virtue of their experience of faith: "through a penetrating understanding of the spiritual realities which they experience, and through the preaching of those who have received through Episcopal succession the sure gift of truth" (*DV* 8).[3]

To grasp the unfolding nature of Tradition, which is necessarily a historical understanding of the ecclesial faith, it is of paramount importance to involve the contribution of the *sensus fidei fidelium* (*LG* 12) and the circularity that binds Tradition and the *sensus fidei* to each other with the inspiration of the Holy Spirit. Indeed, it is "with the help of the Holy Spirit" (*DV* 8) and "by the power of the Holy Spirit" (*GS* 43) that the Church remains faithful to the Paschal witness of the Apostles, preserving its original generative power and, at the same time, opens itself to the contingencies of today, directing its own steps along new paths of proclaiming the Gospel.[4]

Keeping in mind the teaching and the conciliar clarifications on the Tradition of the Church is indispensable for grasping the invaluable contribution of what Pope Francis sets out in *Fratelli Tutti*.

In fact, the pope expresses his intention unequivocally right from the opening lines of the encyclical: to look at our all being siblings as a *dynamic* and *open* reality constitutes a path of

---

[3] Commenting on the dynamics of the Magisterium of the Church, Karl Rahner states: "In this faith, in this history of faith, in this evolution of dogma on which the Magisterium concretely depends, all the members of the Church cooperate, each in his or her own way, by their lives, by their confession, by their prayer, by their concrete decisions, and by their theology. And all that they do in this sense is by no means the mere implementation of truths and norms derived from the Magisterium" (K. Rahner, *Nuovi Saggi*—our translation). Cf. K. Rahner, "Esperienza dello Spirito Santo," in *Nuovi Saggi. Dio e Rivelazione,* vol. 7, Edizioni Paoline, Roma 1980, 277–308.

[4] Cf. J. A. Möhler, *L'unità nella Chiesa, cioè, il principio del Cattolicesimo, nello spirito dei Padri della Chiesa dei primi tre secoli,* Città Nuova, Roma 1969, 139–142.

proclaiming and transmitting the Gospel for the Church today. Handing over the crucified and Risen Christ to new generations, to the people of our time, is no longer convincing as a simply "informative" effort, aimed at communicating the truths of faith concerning the mystery of the living God. Rather, evangelizing today involves the posture and attitudes of believers in relation to the world and their fellow human beings. It is a question of a *relational* style.

In this period of history, the living Tradition of the Church is called to share the deposit of the faith through the life and quality of the relationships that the baptized establish daily with those they encounter in their daily lives.

Indeed, as the first area of engagement for the laity, Vatican II indicated not the Christian community, but rather the "secular" world (*LG* 31). Because of their own particular character, lay people are called to offer a witness that—like yeast in dough—serves to leaven civil society. Obviously, this approach does not exclude dedicated participation in the life of the Church. Rather, it orients the meaning and direction of participating in the Christian community; the laity are called to act "outside" the community, to make Christ present in the world, seeking the Kingdom of God wherever they live out their lives, day after day. What defines the Catholic laity, then, is the capacity to transmit the Gospel in the context of daily life, following the creativity of the Holy Spirit, offering others such occasions of encounter with the Risen One that occur when relationships are marked by loving care and active charity.

In creating music, a composer imagines a work and places in the overture all the motifs that will subsequently be developed. Likewise, Pope Francis starts his reflection on social coexistence as our being siblings and friends with a vision of the Tradition of the Church grounded in the richness of the Council's teachings, to which we have alluded above; "the sign of the times" is an understanding of the faith that advances by way of relationships, becomes unconditionally welcoming to all, and creates bonds of social friendship and our all being siblings.

Two general objections

Fratelli Tutti looks to the figure and life of Saint Francis of Assisi and lets itself be inspired by his capacity for dialogue and by his universal aspiration to "siblings all" that animated the faith, words, and missionary work of the "Poor One" or *Poverello* of Assisi.

If the command Saint Francis received from the crucifix of San Damiano—"Go and repair my house"—constitutes the starting point from which the Holy Father drew light for the Apostolic Exhortation *Evangelii Gaudium*, just as the *Canticle of the Creatures* does for the Encyclical *Laudato Si'*, in *Fratelli Tutti* he refers, right from the choice of the title, to a passage from the *Admonitions* in which Saint Francis exhorts "siblings all" to turn their gaze to Christ.[5] It is an invitation addressed to the whole universe; for Saint Francis, all creatures—both living and inanimate—and all human beings—men and women, young and old, lay and clergy, baptized and non-Christian—are recognized as *fratres omnes*, as "siblings all," because we have seen the face of the one Father of all, through the saving work accomplished in Christ Jesus.

The theme of human belonging and solidarity is one of the main threads that run through the Magisterium of Pope Francis. We can think of chapter four of *Evangelii Gaudium*, in which the social effects of a joyful proclamation of the Gospel are made explicit, or chapter five of *Laudato Si'*, in which some lines of orientation are given for a world that is more just toward people and more respectful of creation.

These magisterial documents open up the horizon within which *Fratelli Tutti* is situated, but it is the *Document on Human Fraternity for World Peace and Living Together* to which it refers explicitly and that provides its formal point of view from which to reflect "together." The meeting that took place on

---

[5] "Let us all, brothers and sisters (*Guardiamo, fratelli tutti . . .*), consider the Good Shepherd who to save His sheep bore the suffering of the Cross." Cf. *Admonitions*, 6, 1 (trans. Pascal Robinson, 1905).

February 4, 2019, in Abu Dhabi, with the Grand Imam of Al-Azhar Ahmad Al-Tayyeb, was defined by Pope Francis himself as "no mere diplomatic gesture" (*FT* 5). Rather, it was an occasion for encounter and joint commitment in favor of humanity, and it represents an epochal turning point in the promotion of interreligious dialogue and a milestone in the construction of a world more of siblings and greater solidarity.[6]

In the opening words of *Fratelli Tutti*, Francis immediately takes note of what might loom as two facile objections to his proposal for a social project based on our all being siblings and friends: exorbitant costs, and the preservation of identity.

The first objection points to the huge expenses and burdens that such a project would require. Thinking about being siblings on a global scale is as ambitious as it is expensive. It conflicts with the interests and laws of a market that has competitiveness as its inescapable premise. Thus, belonging is a luxury that only a few can afford!

Pope Francis responds to this first consideration by recalling the episode of the encounter between the *Poverello* of Assisi and the Egyptian Sultan al-Malik al-Kamil. This moment in the life of Saint Francis becomes a paradigm of meaning and an opportunity to dispel any reticence about the "convenience" of a social project that is inspired by our universally being siblings. The scarce means available did not dissuade the begging saint from carrying out his proposal: to visit the other, far away, a stranger.

---

[6] So much so that in mentioning the event, Pope Francis points to the Document as a text that informs and motivates the Encyclical *Fratelli Tutti* (*FT* 5). Thus the *Document on Human Fraternity for World Peace and Living Together* must be understood as a hermeneutical principle by which we are able to rethink many aspects of the social doctrine of the Church, since it is only by truly encountering those who are different from us that we can emerge from the restrictive posture of constantly trying to convince others that we are right. This Pope Francis reiterates in *FT* 29 when he discusses some of the issues that suffer from an "unacceptable silence on the international level," in particular insecurity and fear; the weakening of spiritual values and our sense of responsibility; shortsighted economic interests; injustice and inequality in the distribution of natural resources; and poverty and hunger.

In his case, poverty, lack of resources, and "differences in language, culture, and religion" did not impede the desire to be close to others. When one is moved by the intention to be "all things to all people" (1 Cor 9:22), rooted in a genuine desire for encounter and relationship, there is no obstacle that cannot be overcome.

Thus, the pope makes it clear that the measure of wealth and the parameters of the economy of profit prove insufficient for "measuring" social relationships. The good knows no limits; it overcomes barriers and gets people on their way. Even more, the creative genius of love, capable of overcoming all resistance and of going beyond what at first glance seems a limitation, is for the believer a supreme expression of fidelity to the Lord (*FT* 3).

The second possible reservation, intending to curb open dialogue and exchange with the other, the different, and the far away, is the defense of one's own identity. This objection shuts down dialogue and encounter with those who are different or far away. In this case, the problem is not the attempt, as such, to safeguard one's own cultural heritage, but rather yielding to the temptation of imposing one's own worldview on others. One can hide behind one's own reasons, impose one's own certainties, fortify convictions and doctrines, in order to defend one's own interests, perhaps disguising them as legitimate reasons or even nonnegotiable principles (*FT* 11). Pope Francis has no qualms in stigmatizing such attitudes as "ideologies of different colors, which destroy (or deconstruct) all that is different" (*FT* 13). Raising the ramparts, erecting walls, and distorting one's own identity—including one's own credo—into a fortified citadel has two direct consequences. First, it has us see ourselves as being under siege, and therefore pushes us to acquire a defensive posture. Second, it leaves out the peripheral realities, since the hardening of one's own positions and the drawing of identity boundaries always require regarding the other as an enemy, even at the cost of forging a false image to justify oneself.

It is paradoxical how the will to pursue a particular truth can end up segmenting and fragmenting it. In this sense, the pope also asks Catholics to renounce engaging with others in an aggressive way. Later in the encyclical, speaking of the grace of Christ as a dynamic of openness and union with the other, he again mentions some believers who think that their greatness "consists in the imposition of their own ideologies upon everyone else, or in a violent defense of the truth, or in impressive demonstrations of strength" (*FT* 92). Rejecting militant attitudes does not mean denying the objectivity of the True, but showing how the splendor of the mystery of Christ manifests itself regardless of any claim to possession. This is the lesson of Saint Francis to his friars, and it is a treasure for every baptized person to receive.

Evangelizing is not imposing a truth. Rather, it means disposing ourselves to a universal openness that follows and imitates the *kenotic* dynamic of the Incarnation, in which the eternal Son took our humanity upon himself, without rejecting any language, religion, or culture, such that "no one is beyond the scope of his universal love" (*FT* 85). In this light, the meeting between Pope Francis and the Grand Imam of Al-Azhar, Ahmad Al-Tayyeb, reflects the visit of Saint Francis to the sultan of Egypt and renews the power of its significance.[7]

Based on these premises, Pope Francis openly expresses his objective: "to contribute to the rebirth of a universal aspiration to fraternity" (*FT* 8) and to aim at the definition of a social doctrine that not only addresses Catholics but can guide everyone.

---

[7] It is this vision of siblings that guides Pope Francis's encounters with the Islamic world and underpins, for example, the joint document signed at Abu Dhabi, which expresses the spirit of *Nostra Aetate*: "The Church regards with esteem also the Moslems. They adore the one God, living and subsisting in Himself; merciful and all-powerful, the Creator of heaven and earth, who has spoken to men. . . . Since in the course of centuries not a few quarrels and hostilities have arisen between Christians and Moslems, this sacred synod urges all to forget the past and to work sincerely for mutual understanding and to preserve as well as to promote together for the benefit of all mankind social justice and moral welfare, as well as peace and freedom" (*NA* 3).

The shadows of a closed world:
Three variables for reading the present time

The practical dimension of the social doctrine proposed as our all being siblings and friends should focus on deeds more than on words. If "Christian convictions" (*FT* 6) remain the basis on which to be guided, the intent is to transcend "particularisms" and invite everyone to engage in the revolution of love, to commit personally to changing things.

Therefore, the practical context, to which Francis often refers, requires first and foremost an accurate examination of current events, investigating their shortcomings objectively and paying attention to their peculiarities. The first chapter of *Fratelli Tutti* analyzes the reasons for the current state of crisis, that is, significant factors of inequality and social injustice.

Pope Francis does not intend to make a "cool and detached description of today's problems" (*FT* 56). Rather, he proposes to initiate a reflection on the present time to unravel some of the many threads that make up its fabric. His intention is to offer a point of view different from common sense, one that is inclusive and can detect today's vulnerabilities. Recalling the opening words of *Gaudium et Spes* makes the point of view clear, with its focus on grasping the joys and hopes, the sorrows and anxieties of today's people, "especially those who are poor or in any way afflicted." This preference for the poor is the defining focus of Christ's disciples, because the sufferings of others find "an echo in their hearts" (*GS* 1) and become a shared experience.

There are three variables applicable to today's world, and their scope is worth making explicit:

1. the collapse of the goals pursued in the past;
2. taking advantage of the present;
3. the declining awareness of history.

Each of these aspects, like pieces of a mosaic, provides a general picture that highlights, on the one hand, the outcome of modernity as the failure of great ideals, and on the other, the destructive effects of consumerism as it frustrates communication between generations (perhaps less evident, but precisely for this reason more alarming).

The collapse of the goals pursued in the past. First of all, Francis focuses attention on the collapse of that common project which allowed modernity to imagine a unified vision of society (*FT* 10–11). The well-known failures in implementing grand and widely shared projects, such as the dream of a united Europe or the integration of Latin American countries, seem to cast a shadow on the realization of goals that go beyond merely nationalistic interests. For Francis, the origin of these failures lies in the failure to guarantee and implement human rights in a universal way.

However, Pope Francis does not stop at a generic assessment that notes our inability to learn from mistakes of the past, but he shows his concern about the new generations.

Young people, the main victims of this general mistrust of long-term projects, are indirectly conditioned by the mistrust of earlier generations.

The result is a sort of disconnect, a break, between the goals set by past generations and the aspirations with which young people tend to imagine the future. The breakdown of communication between generations is a matter of cultural inheritance; justice, solidarity, and the common good no longer fit into that description of the meaning of life that describes someone's life as good and worth living. Rather, the myths of success, of self-affirmation, seem to constitute the only valid and effective narratives for achieving personal fulfillment and satisfaction.

Taking advantage of the present. Onto this weakening of the communal dimension of existence is grafted the ruthless logic of globalization. The current economic model, aimed at maximizing profits, benefits from the pulverization of the sense of belonging to a community and the fragmentation of identities. The economy of profit, on the one hand, instrumentalizes individual needs, pushing them toward a selfish radicalization;

on the other hand, it uses conflicts at the "local" level to exacerbate tensions, disagreements, and vested interests (*FT* 12).

Pope Francis recalls the schism between individual and human community (*FT* 31) as a loss of memory and of historical awareness (*FT* 13–14). This shows how humanity has not learned much from the tragedies of the twentieth century (*FT* 13). Instead of progressing toward a fairer and more united world, a new setback is approaching; conflicts are escalating and setting the stage for "a real 'third world war' fought piecemeal" (*FT* 25). Making individuals lonelier and less rooted in their own context, disconnecting young people from the communities they belong to, and orienting them toward a self-referential lifestyle—all of this is aimed at making them more efficient consumers. At the mercy of their own impulses, they seek to define themselves on the basis of superfluous needs the market imposes as "necessary." Burdened with the discouraging reality of increasingly isolated individuals, distracted consumers, and alienated spectators of today's ugliness, the siblings' path emerges as the only way out of an asphyxiated condition and solipsistic existence.[8]

The declining awareness of history. Grouping people into anonymous "masses" has become the program and objective of the global economy, and it is mainly the new generations who are paying the price. Pope Francis explains how this mindless way of planning is manifested in "forms of cultural colonization" that flatten differences and uniform everything to a hypothetical "standard" model.

A kind of "deconstructionism" (*FT* 13) is underway that aims to dissolve historical awareness and undermine the shared memory of past events. Keeping in mind what was said earlier about the breakdown of communication between generations, there's a twofold attack with one and the same objective: to

---

[8] In the light of the Christian Tradition, this tendency toward individualism can be defined as "concupiscence" (*FT* 166), which can only be overcome by opening to a relationship with God that allows us to break out of the constraints of our own petty interests.

confine the individual to the immediate, the present. Indeed, without a "frame" or "background," no impulse can be read and interpreted. Macro-history, which offers a comprehensive and shared understanding of long-term historical facts, and micro-history, which is composed of the short-range experiences and legacy of the elders,[9] allow new generations to contextualize their "feelings" and use a hermeneutic that frees their instincts from the despotism of "everything, right away" which makes them easy prey for consumerism (*FT* 14).

A homily referred to in a footnote and given by Chilean Cardinal Raúl Silva Henríquez[10] provides an additional insight: the loss of structured cultural identity leads to moral degradation. If values—transmitted by education—are lost, then the basic points of reference, indispensable for discerning how concretely

---

[9] Pope Francis has dedicated a great deal of attention to the plight of the elderly, sounding the alarm bells regarding their marginalization from family and social life and its dramatic consequences. During his years as Archbishop of Buenos Aires, he said: "Furthermore, the elderly are also abandoned, and not only to the precariousness of their material well-being. They are abandoned because of our selfish inability to accept their limitations, which reflect our own limitations. They are abandoned to the numerous pitfalls that must be overcome today to survive in a civilization that does not let them be active participants, have a voice, or serve as an example, because the consumerist model dictates 'only youth have any use, and only the youth can enjoy.' These elderly people are the very ones who, in society as a whole, should be a fount of wisdom of our people." J. M. Bergoglio, *Only Love Can Save Us,* 87.

[10] Raúl Silva Henríquez (1907–1999) was the Archbishop of Santiago de Chile, created a cardinal by Pope John XXIII in 1962. He was a tireless defender of human rights, the violation of which became systematic in his native Chile under the military dictatorship of Augusto Pinochet. Pope Francis honored Cardinal Silva Henríquez with these words: "Here I cannot fail to mention Santiago's great bishop, who in a *Te Deum* once said: "If you want peace, work for justice" . . . And if someone should ask us: "What is justice?" or whether justice is only a matter of "not stealing," we will tell them that there is another kind of justice: the justice that demands that every man and woman be treated as such." Pope Francis, *Homily at the Mass for Peace and Justice*, O'Higgins Park, Santiago de Chile, January 16, 2018; cf. Cardinal Raúl Silva Henríquez, *Homily at the Ecumenical Te Deum*, September 18, 1977.

to act, get scattered and everything becomes permissible, because everything is possible.

Deconstructionism works to remove the constraints and fixed points that are necessary for anchoring persons to the community to which they belong. Ethical and spiritual values, a sense of responsibility (*FT* 29), and moral teachings, in fact, connect personal action with community experience. To denigrate and weaken them transforms young people into compulsive consumers, totally uninterested in what lies behind the means of production, such as the depletion of natural resources and the exploitation of workers in poor countries. To counter this trend and promote the good, "every society needs to ensure that values are passed on; otherwise, what is handed down are selfishness, violence, corruption in its various forms, indifference and, ultimately, a life closed to transcendence and entrenched in individual interests" (*FT* 113).

Dissolving history, discrediting elders' experience, also allows words to be emptied,[11] stripping them of the depth of what humanity has already known and struggled for: democracy, freedom, justice, and humanity (*FT* 110). Without historical awareness, it is easier to distort their meaning and use them to justify any kind of ideological discourse.

Communication, too, has to reckon with the changes brought about by globalization and the advent of the digital age, discovering new pitfalls that are totally unknown and unprecedented in human history. For example, we find ourselves dealing with intimacy in an almost paradoxical way; that is, we keep others at a distance but then spy on their every thought or gesture on social media (*FT* 42). The new generations seem unprepared to assess the risks of this excessive publicizing of private life, and the right to intimacy finds itself seriously compromised.

---

[11] Like snakes that molt, shedding off their old skin, meaning slips from words, as if their significance had become tired, old-fashioned, and irrelevant. Cf. U. Morelli, "Incontrarsi. Imperfezione e poetica dell'enunciazione," in *Dialogo dunque sono: come prendersi cura del mondo*, ed. L. Becchetti, P. Coda, and L. Sandonà, Città Nuova, Roma 2019, 18–19.

Digital relationships cannot replace the bonds mediated by physical presence, by being together "in person" and mutually. We need to recover our sensitivity to the body language of those we meet. Social media only give "an appearance of sociability," but they are not enough for building genuine friendship. Their limitation is false appearance; they seem to multiply contacts with others, but in the end, they only multiply the projections of an "I" turned in on itself. It is precisely the ephemeral immateriality characterizing digital interactions that lends itself to amplifying hatred and aggression, for behind the screen of an electronic device, one feels free to launch insults and offenses (*FT* 44).

The need for a common project

Fueling conflict, mutual suspicion, and the logic of confining and denigrating the other serve not only the economics of profit but also the manipulation of political debate. In this sense, *Fratelli Tutti* states: "Our world is trapped in a strange contradiction: we believe that we can 'ensure stability and peace through a false sense of security sustained by a mentality of fear and mistrust'" (*FT* 26).

The loss of a common vision and project, which would orient politics and economics toward shared objectives, not only makes it more difficult to reduce the distances and bridge the gap between wealth and poverty (*FT* 15), but it also leads one to think that it is absurd to imagine that a viable alternative is possible (*FT* 16). Thus, Francis states without hesitation that "the dream of working together for justice and peace seems an outdated utopia" (*FT* 30). The high aspiration of *Fratelli Tutti* is never hidden. The pope says that he is well aware that his statements will be branded as "utopic," but he has already foreseen such criticism and it is not enough to stop him from speaking out with *parrhesia* (boldness). Rather, we must admit that utopia stands as a critique of reality and can be a useful tool for breaking through to new horizons. To push "beyond" utopia means setting out to look for new ways to change the present.

We need, then, to change our approach and accept the urgency of building a "we" that inhabits our common home. Certainly, this about-face goes against the interests of today's economy, which always appear "particular." In order to build together, the pace must slow down. We must patiently and persistently dispose ourselves to encounter and exchange, to bring to the table of decision-making those who are usually kept out of the picture. Stopping to think, to dialogue, and to meditate before choosing and building a more inclusive future, however, is precisely what the consumerist economy tends to avoid. Its frenetic pace of production and ever-accelerating pace of commercial and financial transactions act as a countervailing force, setting an agenda that allows no delay or slowdown (*FT* 17).

The crisis of modernity, and the very essence of secularism, consist, on the one hand, in the disappearance of a "common world,"[12] that is, as a loss of universally shared values, and on the other, in the "banality of evil"; it does not matter if we exploit people or poison nature, what matters is to grow the wealth of a country.[13] The (false) consciousness of economic technocracy is self-absorbed, because it justifies the means by foreseeing the value at the end.

The cult of growth is the fulfillment of the colonization of our imagination, to the point that it seems impossible for the world to function differently from the way it is proposed.[14] *Laudato Si'* offers an accurate picture of the ecological crisis, a lucid diagnosis of the situation, while *Fratelli Tutti* carefully analyzes its causes and denounces those who are responsible.

---

[12] Cf. H. Arendt, *Vita attiva. La condizione umana*, Bompiani, Milano 1988, 58.

[13] Cf. A. Berthoud, *Une Philosophie de la consommation. Agent économique et sujet moral*, Presses universitaires du Septentrion, Villeneuve-d'Ascq 2005.

[14] Cf. S. Latouche, *Come reincantare il mondo. La decrescita e il sacro*, Bollati Boringhieri, Torino 2020, 30–37.

Francis points to the "throwaway culture" as one of the obstacles to true integral development. Appropriation, depredation, privatization, and exploitation are dynamics intrinsic to the throwaway logic of today's economy. The excluded are perceived as the "collateral damage" (*LS* 49) of a socio-economic system that is supported by conniving and inadequate politics that intervenes only when the harmful effects on people and the environment are now irreversible (*LS* 21).

A sort of "economic Darwinism" has introduced a criterion of ruthless selectivity in which a few hoard large portions of resources to the detriment of many. The idea that there is an "expendable" part of humanity creeps in as an inescapable necessity. Not only food, clothing, and optional goods, but also human beings, are subject to the rules of productivity (*FT* 18). Those most exposed to this way of seeing things are the more vulnerable: human life itself in its beginning and ending moments, the "unborn" and the "dying." Those about to be born and the elderly represent the principal "victims" of today's economic system (*FT* 19).

Growth is no longer an indicator of effective and integral human development. It is the separation between these two terms of the equation—growth and development—that generates the need for waste. Wealth increases without fairness. On the contrary, it generates new poverty and at a high price to pay: the majority of humanity is excluded from decent living conditions.[15] A kind of "schism" sets in between individual well-being and human happiness (*FT* 31), and this feeds on contempt for others. The resurgence of various forms of racism and intolerance is proof that progress, based on growth without development, is a deceptive mirage.

There is a close link between inequality and violence, as it is always in legitimizing asymmetrical relationships that various forms of coercion are deemed permissible.

---

[15] Cf. E. Bazzanella, *Oltre la decrescita. Il tapis roulant e la società dei consumi*, Abiblio, Trieste 2011, 97–110.

Saint Paul VI's *Populorum Progressio* considers development as good *if* it is understood in terms of social justice and peace. Likewise, Benedict XVI's *Caritas in Veritate* legitimizes the market economy *if* seen as welfare for all. However, the idea that development can incorporate social justice by trying to make the economy moral has in some ways proven naive. The increase in gross domestic product (GDP) *per capita*, though an undeniable fact, does not always indicate respect for fundamental human rights. Reducing a person's life to the corresponding amount of GDP annihilates the difference between material progress and moral progress: the good merges with the useful, being is identified with having.

From when economics became a science, that is, since its measure became the objective value of profit, there has been a gradual separation from any ethical concerns. Utilitarianism feeds off the idea that maximizing one's own interest should cause no qualms, even at the cost of trampling on the rights of others.[16]

In Francis's Magisterium, one perceives a difference compared to the approach of his predecessors. It is no longer a question of *moralizing* the economy, of making capitalism more compassionate and "caring," of calling for more crumbs to fall from the rich man's table (Lk 16:19–31), and then of legitimizing and tacitly "blessing" its innate logic of sacrifice. It is not enough to prevent the market from being guided negatively (*CiV* 33) and assure that profit is driven by good ends (*CiV* 21). Nor is it enough to make a generic appeal for corporate responsibility (*CiV* 38; 46) or simply tone down the excesses of the "technocratic paradigm."

Rather, it is necessary to oppose or counter the concupiscent penchant or propensity for selfishness—concupiscence is "the human inclination to be concerned only with myself, my group, my own petty interests" (*FT* 166) that underlies a certain

---

[16] Cf. F. Totaro, "I rischi dell'economismo buono. Una critica etico-filosofica," in *Etica e forme di vita*, ed. A. Da Re, V&P, Roma 2009, 203–215.

socio-economic logic and its practical choices. "It is a matter of redefining our notion of progress" (*LS* 194), of totally changing what underlies a certain socio-economic logic and its practical choices (*FT* 166). "It is a matter of redefining our notion of progress" (*LS* 194), of totally changing the framework (*FT* 179) and way of seeing the world, and of radically rethinking the economic model—"otherwise we would be dealing merely with symptoms" (*LS* 9). Only "an economy that is an integral part of a political, social, cultural, and popular program directed to the common good" (*FT* 179) can escape the destructive dictates of technocratic economics (*FT* 175). It would not be really worthy of humankind for development not to respect and promote human rights, personal and social, economic, and political rights, including the rights of nations and peoples (*LS* 93; *FT* 173).

Anthropological reductionism and human rights: *The dignity of the person as the frontier of the future*

Disenchantment, modernity's most recent result, has produced profound disillusionment with its myth of the omnipotence of progress. This disappointment has unfortunately not yet led to a downsizing of presumption, but to a "cool, comfortable, and globalized indifference" (*FT* 30) that leads to a blind cynicism about the needs of others. Technology is advancing exponentially, but one cannot speak of "progress" if a large portion of humanity pays the price and remains cut off from it. This distorted idea of growth dehumanizes our social coexistence. Deceptive measurement of poverty—which employs parameters that are not always able to monitor reality in a factual and reliable way—attempts to reassure us by downplaying the effects of poverty or camouflaging them behind an aura of acceptability.[17]

The profit-driven economic model is ideologically supported by various anthropological reductionisms. This leads not only

---

[17] Cf. G. Rist, *L'Économie ordinaire entre songes et mensonges*, Presses de Sciences Po, Paris 2010.

to less fairness on the material level, such as lack of access to basic necessities, but even undermines the universality of human rights (*FT* 22). Human dignity is not guaranteed to all: slavery still exists today in many nations; the condition of women is far from equal to that of men; many children are denied the right to a childhood; human trafficking provides criminal organizations with a constant supply of people to employ in illicit activities, such as the exploitation of labor or the scourge of sex trafficking. Reduced to objects, these people are deprived of their original dignity as creatures made in the image and likeness of God.

Populist regimes and supporters of economic liberalism are proving increasingly skillful in deflecting public attention to the phenomenon of migration. The misuse of information and data has proven, in many cases, to be a winning strategy for easily gaining public support. However, such misreadings of reality, generously seasoned with demagogy, depict the phenomenon of migration falsely as an undue invasion and misleadingly project catastrophic scenarios as likely to follow a tolerant acceptance of newcomers.

The sense of fear and frustration that such narratives generate in the public is deliberately heightened. Appealing to "gut instincts" and "knee-jerk reactions" and playing on negative emotions such as exasperation and rage, the reconstruction of the facts leaves out those who are directly responsible for the economic systems that bases the opulence of the West on the impoverishment of developing countries. Hiding the real causes at the roots of migratory flows is a deceptive sleight of hand at the service of the global economy and its interests.

From misinformation flows an inadequate way of dealing with the issue on the part both of politics with its promises and proposals and of the public with its fears and instinctive reactions. Excessive information does not lead to a greater knowledge of reality, nor does "a flood" of it "at our fingertips . . . make for greater wisdom" (*FT* 50).

Populist arguments propose two solutions to the problems associated with migration: limiting aid to poor countries, and imposing austerity measures.[18] Such political engineering starts from an abstract point of view and overlooks the real facts of suffering and the drama of people forced to migrate (*FT* 37). This happens when one observes the world through the keyhole of special interests; the way one looks on others is limited and unidirectional.

If politics is sometimes guilty of an excess of reason, the way in which public opinion deals with the problem of migration commits the opposite error: it lacks rationality and lets itself be guided by mere instinct (*FT* 41).

Pope Francis invites European countries to recover those tools and resources, already theirs by virtue of history and tradition, to reaffirm the dignity of the human person. Europe is, indeed, the cradle of humanism, and its cultural heritage contains the values necessary to defend and preserve the centrality of the human person as a subject of rights and responsibilities. It is on the basis of this heritage that politics must engage in mediating between European citizens and migrants, so that the protection of the rights of some does not undermine protecting those of others (*FT* 40). Quoting Benedict XVI, *Fratelli Tutti* states that work must also be done to guarantee people "the right not to emigrate, that is, to remain in one's homeland" (*FT* 38).

Pope Francis asks the citizens of Europe to go beyond the natural instinct of self-defense, in order to integrate within themselves "a creative openness to others" (*FT* 41). He reminds Catholics that Christian faith is irreconcilable with attitudes that harm human dignity, such as refusing to welcome others or consenting to the marginalization of migrants, stigmatizing them as "excluded" (*FT* 39). In order to overcome any defensive

---

[18] Cf. I. Bifarini, *I coloni dell'austerity. Africa, neoliberismo e migrazioni di massa,* Youcanprint, Roma 2018; cf. L. Mola, "Profili di compatibilità delle misure di austerità con la Carta dei diritti fondamentali dell'Unione europea," in *La crisi del debito sovrano degli stati dell'area euro. Profili giuridici,* ed. G. Adinolfi and M. Vellano, G. Giappichelli Ed., Torino 2013, 81–104.

attitudes dictated by fear, it is necessary to be "reasonable," that is, to exercise the very human quality of intelligence that leads one to read facts and dominate impulses. For believers, this means assuming for oneself the rationality of the Incarnate *Logos,* for it is love that sets us above the animal level and allows us to understand the true reasons of the other.

5.

SCRUTINIZING THE PRESENT:
LETTING THE WORD OF GOD ENLIGHTEN US

(*Fratelli Tutti*, ch. 2)

Listening to the Word of God is essential to judge contemporary history evangelically and to find solutions to the challenges of today.

Pope Francis dedicates the second chapter of *Fratelli Tutti* to the parable of the Good Samaritan (Lk 10:25–37), arguing that it is necessary to pause and meditate, to "search for a ray of light" in the Gospel, "before proposing a few lines of action" (*FT* 56).[1]

After analyzing the current situation (*FT*, ch. 1), this Lucan passage illuminates the present and invites us to change our way of looking at the reality in which we are immersed. Above all, it is an opportunity to reflect on the widespread "illiteracy of care" that afflicts contemporary society, which is characterized by indifference toward the neighbor and a sort of unconscious disinterest in the needs and fragilities of others.

Confronting ourselves with the demands of the Gospel makes it possible to relaunch hope and to recover the aspiration

---

[1] In this way of proceeding, we recognize a concrete example of the *inductive method*: observing reality, discerning the facts in the light of the Word of God, and acting in a way that brings faith and life together.

to fullness that dwells in the human heart, opens it up, and makes room for the presence of the Other and of others (*FT* 54–55). A different way of "sensing" and "perceiving" the other takes hold within us, one in which the love of Christ provides new eyes to see and recognize—in the stranger whom we run into along the way—a sibling to welcome, support, and get standing upright.

A parable for everyone:
The Word of God transcends every border

From the first lines of *Fratelli Tutti*, the Holy Father makes clear his strong desire to address all people without distinction, regardless of any difference in religion or culture. In the second chapter of the encyclical, the choice of the Lucan passage seems to have this same intention: the Gospel parable stands as a narrative that is open to all, that is, capable of speaking to every person of good will and to anyone who lets himself or herself be addressed by it.

It is worth making explicit what the opening lines of this second chapter seem to suggest: the parable is the Word of God and as such transcends any confessional boundaries. It speaks to everyone, even to whoever stands before it without recognizing and welcoming it as the Gospel, including someone who approaches it as any literary text or edifying story.

However, in recalling the Old Testament background of the parable (*FT* 57–60), the encyclical seems to contextualize this claim of a universal addressee in the perspective of an overall understanding of the event of Revelation. In fact, there's emphasis on how in the Bible, God's love becomes manifest according to a specifically pedagogical intention: God reveals his love progressively, as a dynamism that moves from the particular to the universal. This movement, this desire of God to reach every person, is inherent in the very *fact* of God's self-communication; his love is inclusive because it reaches out "to all" (1 Thess 3:12).

Therefore, to expand one's heart so as not to exclude the stranger, "to embrace the foreigner" (*FT* 61), is, on the part of God, the peak or summit of God's "expressing himself" in Christ and, on the part of humanity, the response of faith with which the disciple enters into the mystery of restitution, of giving all back: "In everything, do to others as you would have them do to you" (Mt 7:12).

In the process by which faith embraces the reality of the present, the pope emphasizes the importance of feelings or the emotional sphere, particularly the power of remembering. In the Bible, God advises the people of Israel not to forget that they were "slave" and "stranger," because remembering one's own past enables one to empathize with those who find themselves living in the same miserable condition (Ex 22:20).

The logic of faith draws strength from the qualities of memory and empathy in the human soul; if we do not identify with the suffering of others, if we do not recognize in their afflictions the pain that we remember experiencing ourselves, then faith remains a disembodied exercise of the mind.

However, when we resonate with the pain of others, we discover that there is a "fundamental law of our being" (*FT* 66): our existence is inseparably linked to that of others. What truly "fulfills" us as human beings is love (*FT* 68), because it is inherent to our very being to pursue the good. Recovering the intrinsically relational dimension of our human nature reveals that in it there is an order (*ordo*): we have been created to find in others the fulfillment of ourselves. To encounter the other is a constitutive moment in becoming an individual and part of the process of becoming who and what we are, even when doing so includes the burden of engaging in an "interior struggle" (*FT* 69).

The commitment to building a more just world, with a fairer and more inclusive social and political order, is not a decision to be superimposed on our nature as a cultural construct but is already inscribed in the depths of being human.

Rediscovering the original truth of our being created "in the image and likeness of God" (Gen 1:26) means understanding ourselves anew in the light of a God who is substantially love in relationship. This implies making a fundamental existential choice that transcends the simple fact of "doing something" for others, because it goes beyond a utilitarian and functionalist conception of life and of what is specifically human, but disposes one to "be someone" for the others, inasmuch as acting in favor of one's neighbor can never be separated from the will to enter into a personal relationship of proximity and closeness (*FT* 67).

A parable of "perception": ## *Converting how we look and see*

The Holy Father's interpretation of the Gospel parable of the Good Samaritan differs from the practically "classical" exegesis of the passage, which has tended to highlight the exemplary attitude of the Samaritan and then encourage the hearers to identify with him. In fact, such an interpretation—centered on the verse "he saw him and had compassion on him" (Lk 10:33)—encourages the reader or listener to be inspired by the figure of the Samaritan and to act by imitating his feelings of pity and his care.

Yet this way of interpreting the parable does not highlight its true nature, which intends to encourage not merely a more "moral" behavior but the conversion of our way of perceiving the other. For this reason, we could call it a parable of *perception,* in the sense that, before any possible gestures and responses of charity, Jesus asks us to transfigure the gaze or look with which we regard our neighbor, starting with a radical change of heart.

The parable does not seek to make us better, but invites us to be "new," to let ourselves be touched by the pain of the other so deeply that we are completely changed by it and so unable to be the same as before.[2] The Lord points to this conversion (*metanoia*) of our perception in the question that he addresses to his interlocutors: "Which of these three, do you think, was a neighbor to the man who fell into the hands of the robbers?" (Lk 10:36).

Transferring the category of "neighbor" from the victim of the robbers to the Samaritan allows Jesus to show us how the encounter with someone who is suffering has a transforming effect on those who allow themselves to be touched by the sufferer's personal drama and get involved. In this light, perceiving the other person as a sibling is never the consequence of a willfulness or "voluntarism" that is self-imposed by imitation and that "from the outside" induces us to act a certain way, but always happens "from the inside," that is, by virtue of the love of God that disposes us to truly be siblings and not only act as such.

A sapiential or wisdom reading of the Lucan parable offers worthwhile points for reflection and helps to ask the right questions, to question oneself in a personal way. The objective is to encourage readers or listeners to let themselves be touched (*FT* 64; 72), not to remain indifferent, but to recognize themselves as protagonists and actors in those processes that give rise to being siblings in society.

The parable sets the stage for the points the pope wishes to convey. Although humanity has marked great achievements and reached goals that were unimaginable a century ago, we have not yet learned the language of being close to the other. We may be capable of caring in our own small way, in the "private" dimension of family relationships or in the restricted circle of our acquaintances, but we are far from having made this a

---

[2] John Paul II in *Sollicitudo Rei Socialis* had already declared that recognizing the dignity of the human person transforms solidarity toward our neighbor into charity. In this sense, it is more than "a feeling of vague compassion or shallow distress at the misfortunes of so many people, both near and far. On the contrary, it is a firm and persevering determination to commit oneself to the common good; that is to say to the good of all and of each individual, because we are all really responsible for all" (*SrS* 38).

wide-reaching social attitude. Delegating "care" to specialized sectors of society leads us to think that it is a responsibility that does not concern us directly, and that there are others who have been designated for specific tasks or duties because they have been endowed with specific competences and roles. Yet, learning the alphabet of care is indispensable for fulfilling ourselves as persons, since reciprocity is a constitutive dimension of human nature.[3]

We must not delegate to others the task of bringing about the change but, rather, be its active interpreters. *Fratelli Tutti* thus denounces the establishment of a causal relationship between the widespread attitude of indifference on the individual level and the perpetration of various forms of injustice on the social level. The conversion of social structures begins "from below"; it happens in the decision to play our part in a spirit of "co-responsibility" (*FT* 78, 77).

A stranger on the road:
Stimulated to abandon disengagement

The individual habit of "passing by" has direct consequences on the lives of others, but most of all, it means not valuing the importance of whoever is down, injured, and humiliated—whether a human person, a people, or the environment. Through the figures of the priest and the Levite, *Fratelli Tutti* stigmatizes the widespread attitude of disinterest toward the needs of others and the ease with which other concerns get put ahead of them, are deemed more urgent or important (*FT* 64).

---

[3] This point is clearly expressed in a passage of *Gaudium et Spes*: "Man's social nature makes it evident that the progress of the human person and the advance of society itself hinge on one another. For the beginning, the subject and the goal of all social institutions is and must be the human person which for its part and by its very nature stands completely in need of social life. Since this social life is not something added on to man, through his dealings with others, through reciprocal duties, and through fraternal dialogue he develops all his gifts and is able to rise to his destiny" (*GS* 25).

There are many ways and means of justification that can be used to absolve one's own callousness, from minimizing the seriousness of one's behavior to blaming the victim. Unmasking these false excuses is indispensable not only for changing one's moral posture, but also for initiating paths of shared solidarity (*FT* 85).

Pope Francis points to the Samaritan who stops to offer aid as an alternative to disengagement. Unlike the other figures, who keep their distance, the Samaritan chooses to set aside his own agenda in order to give priority to the injured man. Taking an interest in the suffering of one's neighbor, allowing oneself to become personally involved, to carry out acts of care, gratuitousness, generosity, and solidarity, is indeed possible. It means, first and foremost, recognizing the other as worthy of receiving attention and being included in our daily life. The Samaritan, after all, made a gift of himself to the other in a concrete way: "He gave him his time" (*FT* 63).

The attitude of indifference testifies to a widespread emotional illiteracy. We have become accustomed to looking away whenever a situation does not involve us directly (*FT* 64). Indeed, not only do we not take on the burdens and dramatic difficulties of others, but we feel a certain annoyance at the inconvenience they represent, "since we have no time to waste on other people's problems" (*FT* 65).

On the ability to recognize the needs of others depends the choice of being "present to those in need of help" (*FT* 81) and of defining paths that orient the economy, politics, social life, and religions toward inclusivity. *Fratelli Tutti* calls for experiences of collaboration to emerge among individuals, institutions, religions, and nations. The Samaritan did not do everything alone but involved others in his action. He becomes a valid example on a personal level and also a social and civil model, because "he summons us to rediscover our vocation as citizens of our respective nations and of the entire world, builders of a new social bond" (*FT* 66).

Likewise, the choices made at the level of international politics—coming to the aid of injured states, lifeless by the side of modernity's road—open up a possible new direction of economic and social planning that is oriented toward promoting humanity and integration, especially of those who have "fallen" (*FT* 77).[4]

True inclusivity does not neglect any aspect of reality, and it pays attention to creation. Even creation, in the light of the *Canticle* of Saint Francis, is to be thought of as *sibling* (*FT* 2). Thus, integrating creation into the regulation of social agreements becomes an expression of Christian action that reflects the logic of our faith and the style of mutual belonging that characterizes the disciples of the Lord Jesus.

Retreating "together" from the logic of the violent: Economy and solidarity

As the famous Latin phrase *tertium non datur* states, there is in fact no "third way" or other option. Either we get our hands dirty, as the Samaritan did, or we take the side of the indifferent passers-by, who find it more convenient to keep their distance (*FT* 69). In other words, the parable of the Good Samaritan seems to offer only one alternative, contrasting two types of people: those who stop, and those who walk by faster. The encounter with the suffering of others is revelatory, is apocalyptic, because it unveils the truth of who we are (*FT* 70).

The parable of the Good Samaritan is applicable not only to individual experiences of life but has much to say about politics and civil society. There is a fundamental option regarding social choices. Nations exist that, like the robbers whom Jesus depicts, plunder other countries, leaving them on the ground, prostrate and bloodied. Other nations, then, go their own way, as if nothing that happens in the world concerns them in any way.

The indifference of the priest and the Levite seems to describe the attitude of countries that "look elsewhere," turning

---

[4] Cf. B. Sorge, *Brevi lezioni di dottrina sociale*, Queriniana, Brescia 2017, 50–53.

their gaze (*FT* 73), focusing on their own economy, adhering more or less tacitly to the ruthless logic of "economic Darwinism." There is a tightening collusion in evil: the robbers who plunder often make like the indifferent passers-by—their focus is solely on their own interests. Likewise, there are those who exploit, and there are those who accept to exist within systems of exploitation. It is downright hypocrisy to condemn the economy of profit in principle and then tacitly accept its rules, consenting to play along (*FT* 75).

This is not a question of attributing blame or condemning those who are guilty of such misdeeds, because it is not difficult to identify those responsible without a shadow of a doubt; "we know them well" (*FT* 72). The parable is not aimed at incriminating anyone but at awakening awareness and conscience.

Escaping the logic of the violent means, first, cultivating a gratuitous "pure and simple desire" (*FT* 77) to come to the aid of those who are prostrate, to extend a hand to those nations that today are forced to succumb to the laws of the global market. It also means abandoning all childishness that refuses responsibility for the choices made out of nationalistic selfishness or that justifies them in the light of a convenient historical determinism.

To help others is to presuppose that there is a common "we" that goes beyond our particularities and that accepts as a criterion of discernment the idea that "the whole is greater than the part" (*FT* 78; cf. *EG* 235). It is in this direction that processes of transformation can be set in motion and action can be taken on the path of "reparation and reconciliation" (FT 78), healing the excesses of a sick society by laying the foundations of a sense of community that can resolve society's contradictions. In this sense, indifference is not countered by individual initiatives, but by "teaming up," joining forces, and pooling resources.

This means renouncing the self-referential style that often raises walls and barriers, cloaking them in historical and cultural justifications and, on the contrary, to be present and become neighborly, letting our sense of responsibility redefine us as "neighbor" to the other. And if reading the parable of the

Good Samaritan points the way to a sibling relationship for all, revealing in our common human nature the foundation of a universal morality, "for Christians the words of Jesus have an even deeper meaning" (*FT* 85). What is specifically Christian is precisely the fact of recognizing the face of Christ in every abandoned and excluded sibling and believing that Christ "shed his blood for each of us and that no one is beyond the scope of his universal love" (*FT* 85).

Pope Francis is not afraid to admit a certain reluctance on the part of the Church in assuming this logic of nonviolence and in embracing what is specifically Christian: recognizing Christ in every sibling who is abandoned or excluded (*FT* 85). Even the historical slowness to reach a straightforward condemnation of slavery reveals the lack of critical awareness and the difficulty of moving in the right direction. Today, however, we have no more excuses. Faith can never justify xenophobic attitudes or discrimination of any kind. Rather, Francis hopes that catechesis and preaching will take up and incorporate the "fraternal dimension of spirituality" (*FT* 86), so as to reaffirm the inalienable dignity of every person.

6.

GENERATING AN OPEN WORLD: DISCERNING AND JUDGING

(*Fratelli Tutti*, chs. 3–4)

After having sketched the framework of a world closed in on itself and having looked in the Word of God for a horizon of meaning so as to emerge from the impasse in which we find ourselves paralyzed, the third and fourth chapters of *Fratelli Tutti* mean to question the present in order to direct concrete action toward a solidary society of siblings.

Certain fundamental themes of the social teaching of the Church—such as the inalienable rights of the human person, the principle of solidarity, and the universal destination of goods—are approached within the framework of a new ethical-moral understanding of charity. In particular, references to Thomistic ontology and French existentialism become the hermeneutical choice through which Pope Francis explores the theme of love as gift, with the intention of opposing the ethical-pragmatic cynicism that springs from a nihilistic vision of human existence[1] and on which the consumerist and throwaway culture heavily draws.

---

[1] Pope Francis envisions the path of siblings all and social friendship as the only possible alternative to the disenchantment that leads us deeper into the "global illusion" that misleads us. The collapse of consumerist ideology

The challenges, writes Pope Francis, move and force us "to see things in a new light and to develop new responses" (*FT* 128). To succeed in this effort—assuming love as the logical, hermeneutical, and practical criterion that informs and structures relationships as well as institutions—means identifying strategies that motivate us to seek the best for the life of the other (*FT* 94).

The dynamism of grace:
The love of Christ that unites us to the neighbor

The first step to take in order to react to the "virus" of indifference is to restore the value of life. The third chapter of *Fratelli Tutti* pushes "beyond" the enclosure produced by individualism, coming to know the beauty of human existence as a web of true and authentic relationships (*FT* 87). It does this by sketching a small treatise of theological anthropology, with the focus on the experience of grace as "charity that God infuses" (*FT* 91).

The opening lines are enough to outline a framework of meaning with very dense implications. If the reference to *Gaudium et Spes* 24 and the quotation from Gabriel Marcel (*FT* 87) refer to a description of the human being as a mystery that is realized in openness and dialogue with others, the quotation from Karol Wojtyla (*FT* 88) refers to the Scholastic notion of grace

---

"will leave many in the grip of anguish and emptiness" (*FT* 36). The very choice of terms—*anguish* and *emptiness*—does not seem at all accidental, but rather constitutes an obvious reference to the thought of the existentialist philosopher J. P. Sartre and his novel *Nausea*. *Fratelli Tutti* compares the thought of Sartre with that of Gabriel Marcel—two radically different and irreconcilable visions of the world and of the human condition. For example, there is a tremendous gap between Sartre's conception of freedom as the human "nothingness of being" and unconditioned choice, and Marcel's understanding of freedom as "creative receptivity" that is open to the essential relationship with God. Cf. L. Aloi, *Ontologia e dramma. Gabriel Marcel e Jean-Paul Sartre a confronto,* Albo Versorio, Milano 2014.

as "a gratuitous or unowed gift of God superadded to nature (*donum Dei naturae indebitum et superadditum*)."[2] The grace of Christ is always "relational" because it fosters "openness and union with others" (*FT* 91). It is charity, love, that God infuses for the fulfillment or perfection of human nature—already willed and created by God as being ontologically disposed to the divine "You"—so that human beings can employ, through the exercise of their freedom,[3] all the potential for good that they have been made to receive. Love is what achieves passing from potential to the actuality of being. Therefore, love makes us exist and subsist. At the same time, love is what permits creating the authenticity of "we" from self-centeredness, because love makes it possible to recognize the other as the "You" that completes and gives meaning.[4]

---

[2] In the *Summa Theologiae*, Saint Thomas presents grace as an infusion of special, divine light, which is ordered to the knowledge of objects that transcend our natural resources, and which is in addition to ordinary "natural illumination." Cf. Thomas Aquinas, *Summa Theologiae* I-II, q.109, a.1; *De veritate*, q.8, a.7. For an overview of the question, see E. Gilson, *The Spirit of Medieval Philosophy* (Notre Dame, IN: University of Notre Dame Press, 1991).

[3] The quotation from Karl Rahner completes this framework, composed of several authoritative sources, by referring to freedom as a determining aspect of the human person. Indeed, Rahner maintains that in the exercise of freedom, the human person inevitably ends up revealing who he or she is and perceiving himself or herself as a being of transcendence. Freedom is the most original experience in which human beings can perceive their own subjectivity—transcendentally and a priori—as a gift that has been entrusted to them and that intrinsically calls upon their responsibility. Cf. K. Rahner, "Esperienza dello Spirito Santo," in *Nuovi Saggi. Dio e Rivelazione,* vol. 7, Edizioni Paoline, Roma 1980, 277–308. For an in-depth discussion of transcendental freedom in Rahner, see: G. Salatiello, *Tempo e Vita eterna. Karl Rahner e l'apertura del pensiero*, E.P.U.G., Roma 2006, 51–58; cf. H. D. Egan, "The Mystical Theology of Karl Rahner," in *The Way* 52, no. 2 (2013): 43–62.

[4] Love is the only dynamic able to expand the meaning of life. Love is an exodus that allows one to go out of oneself and be liberated from the tyranny of one's own selfish needs; love is an ecstasy that leads to "a fuller existence" (*FT* 88) in relationships.

Therefore, love is the only force that is capable of weaving "hospitable" bonds[5] and generating a society open to integration (*FT* 88–90). Referring to an expression of Saint Thomas Aquinas, the pope explains that the love of Christ is this movement that directs to the good and moves us to turn our attention to our neighbors, considering them precious, seeking the best for their life. Love implies something more than a series of beneficial actions (*FT* 94) in that it leads to "being good" and not only to "doing good things" (*FT* 95). Love encourages us to overcome utilitarian morality, in which the pursuit of good refers primarily to oneself and not to the other. Love, on the contrary, keeps moral action gratuitous and free from prioritizing one's own private interest (*FT* 102).

This inclination toward the good of the other is what Pope Francis calls "openness" (*FT* 95). It is not only geographical, but especially existential; it is the capacity to broaden one's sphere of interests, so as to reach out to those who would not usually be within it (*FT* 97). In other words, it is that disposition of the heart that encourages the involvement and participation of others, especially the "hidden exiles"—all those who live in a prolonged condition of precarity in society, as if they were perpetually foreigners or strangers (*FT* 98).

In this context, a general principle of validity emerges that Pope Francis already mentioned in his commentary on the parable of the Good Samaritan (*FT* 71): the criterion of love as transcending the limits of the self applies as much to the individual as it does to a whole nation (*FT* 96). From individual morality, we pass to social ethics,[6] from the particular

---

[5] *Fratelli Tutti* cites the *Rule* of Saint Benedict (*FT* 90), which teaches that hospitality is the attitude of welcoming the neighbor that leads to transcending oneself, because it is the sign of a heart that is transformed by the loving presence of God. Cf. Benedictus Casinensis, *La Regola di san Benedetto e le regole dei Padri*, ed. S. Pricoco, Mondadori, Milano 1995, Cap. LIII, 233–236.

[6] The concluding part of the chapter explains that this movement from the individual level to the social level—to the ethics of "we"—also pertains

to the universal, without thereby creating any category of discontinuity or finally endorsing a division between "public" and "private" that in fact legitimizes a "compartmentalized morality."

In the final analysis, the pope does not propose an "authoritarian and abstract universalism" (*FT* 100), but indicates as a goal the appropriation of a social coexistence that aspires to bring all social actors into harmony and that leaves no one behind or confined to the margins. This way of thinking about society is inspired by the Gospel ideal of universal communion. It is with the understanding that in *Fratelli Tutti* this proposal is put forward in a way that can be shared by all, including nonbelievers and those who belong to other religions.

Extending the meaning of "being siblings": Making the rights of the person and of peoples truly universal

There is no doubt that the foundations of the Western world, in its current socio-political and economic configuration, rest on those Enlightenment ideals that were famously summarized in the iconic motto "liberty, equality, and fraternity."[7] By setting "siblings all" as its focus and theme, *Fratelli Tutti* could not avoid inspiring a comparison, however veiled, with the formulation of these principles as solemnly expressed in the *Declaration of the Rights of Man and the Citizen* (1789).[8]

In this legal text, drafted during the French Revolution, *freedom* is defined as the attribute of the individual citizen "to

---

to the relationship among countries. Pope Francis again asks us to reflect on an "ethics of international relations" (*LS* 51; *FT* 126) and "a global ethic of solidarity and cooperation" (*FT* 127).

[7] Cf. A. Martinelli, M. Salvati, and S. Veca, *Progetto 89. Tre saggi su libertà, uguaglianza, fraternità,* Il Saggiatore, Milano 2009, 34–51.

[8] Cf. *Declaration of the Rights of Man and the Citizen, 1789 and 1793,* Department of History, University of Liverpool, 1985.

be able to do whatever he wants, as long as it does not harm others" (art. 5), so as to underline resolutely the right of the individual to self-determination, that is, not to be bound by pre-determined obligations and duties that come from being born in a given social class.

Equality, on the other hand, refers primarily to the legal system of the state, since it derives from the fact that the law—"an expression of the general will" (art. 6) of the citizens—is the same for all, regardless of rank or social status.

Finally, *fraternity* is expressed as that sense of solidarity that is established among citizens when they recognize that they are "free and equal" (art. 1). In this sense, full sovereignty is granted to a people and nation whose citizens recognize themselves as equal members (art. 3).

The *Declaration of the Rights of Man and the Citizen* is considered one of the highest expressions of the recognition of human dignity. It is as an indispensable reference point for the drafting of numerous charters and constitutions, and for all democracies that have been formed following the Second World War. It is not surprising, then, that the Universal Declaration of Human Rights promulgated by the General Assembly of the United Nations in 1948 took the *Declaration* of 1789 as its model and even quoted some parts verbatim.[9]

Fratelli Tutti seems to throw out a question: what do words such as *liberty, equality,* and *fraternity* mean for us today? To be more explicit, what consequences does the emergence of a global marketplace have for the international protection of human rights, both of individuals and of peoples? If we consider

---

[9] Like the *Declaration* of 1789, the UN Declaration reflects the needs of the time, but thanks to its firm and fundamental principles, over the past decades it has been able to win battles in the field of human rights. It should be noted that the greatest innovations introduced with respect to the *Declaration* of 1789 are the abolition of slavery and recognition of the rights of women (such as the right to autonomy or motherhood). Of equal importance is the recognition of the rights to work, family, and citizenship. Cf. *La Dichiarazione dei diritti umani nel diritto internazionale contemporaneo*, ed. S. Tonolo and G. Pascale, G. Giappichelli Editore, Torino 2020.

the great atrocities committed against human dignity that we still witness today—genocide, torture, the death penalty, fundamentalism, racism—can we really maintain the "universality" of human rights as extending equally to all people?[10] Francis points out that "respect for individual liberties" and "a certain administratively guaranteed equality" (*FT* 103), while indispensable conditions for affirming the rights of the person and of peoples, are not sufficient to guarantee that they will effectively be enjoyed by all.

From the pope's point of view, it is necessary to start from a "consciously cultivated" fraternity (*FT* 103) in order to shed light on what freedom and equality are and how they are to be understood. Being siblings is more than a generic sense of solidarity based on the common recognition of a national identity, since it precedes and goes beyond the rights and duties on which civil coexistence is established. Being siblings is based on the recognition of the fundamental equality of all people. Thus, being siblings is founded on natural law even before being enshrined in any society's law.

In this light, equality cannot be affirmed only in principle, as an abstract concept.[11] Rather, equality must be the result of a "conscious and careful cultivation of fraternity" (*FT* 104). This calls for education in recognizing the other as similar and equal, and also the manifest expression of political will and concerted effort of all those who are responsible for education and formation. Otherwise, any idea of equality based exclusively on positive law, on the basis of defining the person as a citizen (*homo societatis*), creates "closed worlds" and treats human relations as a contract between business "associates" (*FT* 104).

Without being siblings, the exercise of freedom shrinks and reduces to autonomy, a weak expression of freedom. The difference between being siblings and any other form of association

---

[10] Cf. A. Cassese, *I diritti umani oggi*, Edizioni Laterza, Roma-Bari 2015.

[11] This clarification at the beginning of chapter 4 (*FT* 128) serves as the basis for all that follows on the theme of immigration.

is marked by the willingness to break out of the twofold illusion that thinking only of oneself is more advantageous, and that the common good is built on the basis of self-interest. To interpret being siblings and equality by giving priority to individual liberties threatens the universality of rights. The same is true of the absolute or unquestionable freedom of the market; that is, the right to enterprise cannot be put before the dignity of the poor or above the environment (*FT* 122). The conclusion the pope reaches is clear: "Individualism does not make us more free, more equal, more fraternal" (*FT* 105).

A "basic acknowledgment": The inalienable right to integral human development

For Francis, when it comes to the meaning of terms such as *freedom, equality,* and *fraternity,* the heart of the matter lies in a "basic acknowledgment" (*FT* 106): attributing value and dignity to the human person regardless of any historical, geographical, cultural, or political factors. This is followed by another declaration, which almost becomes a prophecy: if every human being is not recognized as having a fundamental and inalienable right to his or her integral development, then "there will be no future either for fraternity or for the survival of humanity" (*FT* 107). Any limitation of this right, as well as any attempt to bind its exercise to certain conditions—for example, a personal determination to "assert or stand up for oneself"—is to be considered a violation.

The right to human development cannot be made subject to any calculation of efficiency, any claim of social utility, that ends up justifying the option of leaving the weaker or less gifted behind (*FT* 108). Rather, the rights of the person must never be interpreted in a way that extracts the individual from the social "we"—otherwise, human rights dissolve into various irresolvable contradictions or aporias. For example, an excessive emphasis on individual freedom, which often ends up triggering a downward spiral of conflict and violence (*FT* 111), is perniciously reductionist. With this broad premise of wanting to extend the meaning of being siblings, and noting the need for a proper interpretation of human rights, the pope revisits in an original way two relevant topics of the social teaching of the Church: the principle of solidarity (*FT* 114–115), and the right to private property (*FT* 118–120).

Regarding the *principle of solidarity*, Pope Francis calls upon the major agencies of education and formation—families, schools, parishes, cultural centers, recreational programs, and so forth—to devote themselves to the "conscious and careful cultivation of fraternity" (*FT* 104). Amid the current crises in education, transmitting the values of freedom, mutual respect, sharing, and inclusion is perhaps the principal form of solidarity that is required. Restoring the chain that transmits the value of the person is a form of social and moral responsibility.

Educating new generations from the earliest age to be siblings helps them to understand that solidarity is a way of situating themselves in time and in life. It is the disposition to feel the other's nearness to the point of "suffering" it. Compassionate living is more than making a gesture of assistance, or the mere fact of doing a good deed, because it entails having the other person's situation at heart. Countering the "throwaway culture" is also a form of social solidarity, because it demonstrates a moral conscience that is sensitive to our common home and the future of humanity (*FT* 117).[12]

Regarding the *right to private property*, Pope Francis underlines that it derives from the principle of the universal destination of created goods (*FT* 120). The pope points out how

---

[12] Various forms of ideology threaten solidarity because they always lead to a struggle against poverty and its diverse causes or roots. However, putting ourselves at the service of others protects us from such distortions, since serving the neighbor means serving not ideas but living persons (*FT* 115).

this was already expressed in a clear and direct way by the Fathers of the Church: if someone lacks what he or she needs, it is because someone else is misappropriating it (*FT* 119). In continuity with the Magisterium of Paul VI and John Paul II, Francis argues that the right to private property is not absolute. It is to be considered "secondary" and "derived" from the universal destination of goods. The right to private property is always accompanied by the primary and prior principle of the subordination of all private property to the universal destination of the earth's goods, and thus the right of all to their use" (*FT* 120, 123).

If we root the right to private property, as well as the rights of the citizens of a state, in the conviction that the goods of the earth belong to everyone, then we realize that "each country also belongs to the foreigner" and that what the earth offers in a given place cannot be denied "to a needy person coming from elsewhere" (*FT* 124). If the criterion of love that transcends the limits of the self is applied to the right to private property and its related rights, then this way of seeing things will have repercussions on the functioning of a state and on international relations. Indeed, every nation is responsible for the development of other countries and for the integral promotion of those who are denied the right to material subsistence and progress, even outside their own borders (*FT* 125). The invitation to overcome bilateralism between countries with advanced economies and countries with emerging economies is a heartfelt appeal for solidarity, "interdependence, and shared responsibility" (*FT* 127), so that everyone may have what is necessary to live decently, in dignity.

Discerning today's global problems according to the criterion of charity and love means stimulating and accompanying processes, not imposing certain approaches. For this it is necessary to change perspective and invert one's point of view so as to look at individual freedom from the viewpoint of being siblings with a shared sense of "we," and, when considering private property, to recognize the prior right of everyone to access the natural goods and resources of the earth.

A heart open to the whole world: Immigration as an opportunity for enrichment and interchange

The fourth chapter of *Fratelli Tutti* is closely linked to the previous one, applying it and deepening it. After affirming that the recognition of the dignity of every human being is the foundation of universally being siblings, Pope Francis calls for a careful examination of all the concrete implications of making such a claim. If we truly validate the equality of all people, then we must address the more complex problems of our times—such as immigration—by assuming this principle not in the abstract but with realism.

If equality is "to find concrete embodiment" or take on flesh (*FT* 128),[13] then the world becomes a place that is open to exchange among countries, and "it matters little whether my neighbor was born in my country or elsewhere" (*FT* 125), because the right of every human being to full fulfillment as a person must also include "the right of all individuals to find a place that meets their basic needs and those of their families" (*FT* 129). As long as it is not possible to guarantee everyone the right *not* to emigrate should they so choose (*FT* 38), then respecting human dignity and ensuring the integral development of migrants requires co-responsibility[14] among the more developed countries so that "the limits of borders" is overcome.

---

[13] The principle of equality is not an abstract concept but "takes flesh" if it follows the logic of the incarnate Word, the concrete universal. In God, the criterion of love that transcends the limits of the self is not abstract but becomes a *fact* in the event of the Incarnation. In the hypostatic union of Christ's human and divine natures, superabundant love is made flesh, becomes concrete and irrevocable solidarity with humanity.

[14] The pope makes the case for a type of *governance* that goes well beyond emergency measures; it coordinates cooperation between states on immigration, providing for comprehensive legislation that enables short-term and long-term planning (*FT* 132).

Pope Francis affirms, however, that it is not enough simply to "welcome"; we must also work to "protect, promote, and integrate" (*FT* 129). This means, from a conception of society in which the foreigner is discriminated against, we must come to understand social coexistence as guaranteeing "full citizenship" (*FT* 131) to everyone. Rather than "implementing welfare programs from the top down" (*FT* 129), it is a matter of offering practical and concrete possibilities for integration: granting visas, humanitarian corridors, access to education and essential services, the protection of minors, religious freedom, family reunification, and so forth (*FT* 130).

Welcoming in order to integrate makes it possible to reach new and richer syntheses, since every exchange in which the other is not wiped out or put down in his or her identity becomes a resource for the civic community, with new lifeblood that revitalizes the world that "grows and is filled with new beauty" (*FT* 148). The examples of the United States and Argentina, and more generally the encounter between the West and the East, show how good it is to think this way (*FT* 133–136).

In the concluding section of this fourth chapter, we see how, when articulating complex concepts, Francis prefers to bring opposing terms together, terms with "an innate tension" between them (*FT* 142).[15] Thus, the pope underlines the "inseparable and equally vital" polarity (*FT* 142) between globalization and localization. In order to achieve an "openness to the world" (*FT* 151) in which no one is forced to succumb to the

---

[15] Francis admires the thought of Romano Guardini, and his *L'opposizione polare* is one of the significant texts of the pope's formative years. Pope Francis has made the art of holding opposing realities, experiences, and sensibilities together in creative tension a distinctive feature of his personal and pastoral reflection. Cf. R. Guardini, *L'opposizione polare: saggio per una filosofia del concreto vivente*. Morcelliana, Brescia 1997; M. Borghesi, *Jorge Mario Bergoglio. Una biografia intellettuale*, Jacabook, Milano 2017; S. Zucal, "Romano Guardini maestro di papa Francesco," in *Vita e Pensiero* 99, no. 6 (2016): 47–54.

logic of the strongest, there are two pitfalls to avoid: forms of massification that flatten differences, and enclosures that narrow views. Turning our gaze to the global is indispensable if we do not want to remain confined to our own backyard, putting up fences that end up trapping us. Vice versa, the global must not engulf what is proper to local realities, namely, domestic and family life in which all experiences of subsidiarity actually take place.

A final pair of opposing terms is related analogically with the previous one, giving it greater depth: the relationship between universal and particular, referring back to the one between dialogue and identity.

Protecting diversity, the plurality of cultures and of identities, is the criterion for being siblings that aspires to a universality that is neither abstract (*FT* 143) nor imposes itself so as to dominate and cancel out diversity (*FT* 144). Truly being siblings does not homogenize but allows one to remain oneself together with others. Otherwise, a "false openness to the universal" "ends up depriving the world of its various colors, its beauty and, ultimately, its humanity" (*FT* 145; 100).

This passage from the particular to the universal, from the local to the global, takes place as a dialogue among everyone while respecting each person's identity, a dialogue that is cordial or sincere,[16] as Pope Francis calls it, a dialogue in which everyone involved is open to seeking the good of the other.

---

[16] The adjective *cordiale* recurs several times in the encyclical (*FT* 87; 146; 195; 274; 283), although not in the English translation. *Cordiale* indicates a way of relating to the other in a spontaneous manner open to feelings of friendship, in which one has the good of the other at heart. In the previous chapter, Francis expresses this sincere search for the promotion and development of others as *benevolentia*, as a strong desire for and inclination toward all that is good and offers the fullness of life (*FT* 112). This further clarifies the healthy polarity that is established between globally being siblings and social friendship. Being siblings seeks the universal good and uses dialogue between nations, characterized by an attitude of benevolence toward others, as its own means or instrument. Social friendship acts within a given society to seek the specific good and protect its own identity.

7.

BUILDING A BETTER AND MORE OPEN WORLD

(*Fratelli Tutti*, chs. 5–7)

The interconnection and interdependence between the themes treated in chapters 5, 6, and 7 of *Fratelli Tutti* make this part of the encyclical a cohesive unit with a multifaceted or polyhedric variety of perspectives and points of reference.

Politics, dialogue, and peace are the main topics. Without ever overlapping or mixing together, they converge to provide a careful description of our present age and sketch the complicated future toward which to look. Pope Francis's aim is to put some of the burning questions of the day to the test of an urgent and realistic examination, removing them from the unstable ground of suspended judgment or convenient indifference.

Francis's analysis reaffirms and relaunches the principles of the Church's social doctrine in view of further developments. On several occasions, the pope emphasizes the urgency that motivates him to tell things as they are and frankly to address those who are directly responsible.

Connecting his reflections on the topic of politics (ch. 5) and those that pertain to peace (ch. 7) is his key theme of dialogue (ch. 6), practically as if to underline the importance and ability to build a better, more just, and fairer world.

In order to cultivate relationships of honest exchange and friendship in a pluralistic society, it is necessary to strive for tolerance and to practice mutual listening. Thus, dialogue becomes the space that opens up among people, where they can encounter one another in a way that neither conceals their differences nor reduces their uniqueness.

In dialogue, politics faces up to the contradictions that have been stirred up within the social fabric and turns them toward sharing, in a constant balancing act between conflict and cooperation, between hospitality and hostility.

Peace, not merely as an absence of war but as planning that is open to the common good, becomes the objective of every honorable politician and of every person of good will.

"Good politics":
Striving for the high ideals of social ethics

The role of politics is of fundamental importance in achieving our all being siblings and social friendship among us.[1] Pope Francis undertakes to explore this theme deeply in chapter 5 of *Fratelli Tutti*, expressing his point of view from the very first lines: when politics is faithful to its own "vocation," it always places itself at the service of the common good (*FT* 154). Otherwise, if it degenerates into a distorted exercise of authority, it betrays its noble aspiration of being good "government by the people" (*FT* 157). This happens, for example, when it gives in to the temptation of populism[2] or to

---

[1] Pope Francis addressed the theme of "good politics" in *Evangelii Gaudium* 222–233, presenting it as a "lofty vocation" and "one of the highest forms of charity" (*EG* 205). Here, four principles emerge that allow politics to be up to its task: ethical tension, secularity, the common good, and a spirit of service. Cf. B. Sorge, "Per una 'buona politica,'" in *La Politica buona*, ed. M. Pennisi and G. LaVanco, Franco Angeli Editore, Milano 2016, 13–19.

[2] The pope notes that a tendency that has been emerging for some time is to consider populism as a valid "key" for interpreting current political events (*FT* 157). This tendency is ultimately "a source of polarization in an

the enticements of neo-liberalism. From Pope Francis's point of view, politics must be evaluated in relation to the poor; how politics treats those groups in society that are vulnerable and at risk is ultimately what reveals whether it is "good" or "destructive." This conviction rebukes not only populism but also neo-liberalism. Both are forms of bad politics: populism because it uses contempt for the weak as a demagogic tool to create a sense of the "we" that is fueled by exclusion; and neo-liberalism because the economic interests of a few are unscrupulously prioritized over the living conditions of entire populations.

Politics is called to renew itself, to recover its good name, and to avoid falling into those media pitfalls into which it frequently stumbles when it pursues superficial consensus (*FT* 161). Instead, it should strive to bring the attention of public opinion back to relevant questions, giving priority to the issues where the future of humanity is at stake. However, this will not be possible unless politics recovers its high ideals of social ethics without which it is difficult to plan for the long term. If, on the one hand, these words echo Argentinian theology of the people,[3] on the other hand we must note their profound continuity with the social doctrine of the Church, especially with the continual search for a "social utopia" that sees transcendent values inspired by Christianity as a guarantee of fundamental freedoms and civil rights.[4]

Pope Francis invites us to focus our attention on the concept of the "people," because he believes that politics would reju-

---

already divided society," to the point of classifying everything in society as "populist" or not (*FT* 156).

[3] Cf. S. Politi, *Teología del pueblo. Una propuesta argentina a la teología latino-americana. 1967–1975,* Castañeda, Buenos Aires 1992.

[4] This echoes Don Luigi Sturzo's intuition of a *popularism* that starts from the grassroots, from the defense of the rights of farmers and the fight against the scourge of labor trafficking, and that constitutes a valid alternative and antidote to populism. Cf. L. Sturzo, *Politica e morale,* Zanichelli, Bologna 1972; cf. A. Di Giovanni, *L'attualità di Luigi Sturzo, pensatore sociale e politico,* Massimo, Milano 1987.

venate itself if it paused more often to reflect on this notion
and gave it its due importance. In fact, if this category were to
be rediscovered in today's political debate, it would broaden
the horizons of an encounter between sides too often simply
defending their own interests. The concept of "people" must
be adequately understood as pluralist unity, as opposed to any
narrow interpretation that restricts its significance to a "mere
sum of individual interests" (*FT* 157).

Francis clarifies that "people" is to be understood neither
as a "logical category," much less a "mystical category," but
rather as a "mythic category" (*FT* 158). What defines a people
as a collectivity—as a communitarian subject from which
flows an ethical-cultural identity—is more easily expressed
and evoked symbolically[5] than by recourse to rationalist and
positivist concepts.

The noun *people* carries an "additional value" that cannot be
quantified or circumscribed. It encompasses several characteristic elements: "human capital," which is the set of ties that make
up the socio-cultural network of a nation; "immaterial goods,"
such as customs and traditions; the heritage of values shared by
a group of people; and the identification of common goals to be
oriented toward when making choices.[6] For these reasons, the

---

[5] The pope's understanding of the notion of a people resonates profoundly
with the thought of the French philosopher Paul Ricoeur. Ricoeur affirmed
that national cultures possess an ethical-mythical core: *ethical* because they
imply values; and *mythical* because they are expressed in symbolic form. Cf.
P. Ricoeur, "Civilisation universelle et cultures nationales," in P. Ricoeur,
Histoire et Vérité, du Seuil, Paris 1955, 286–300.

[6] Geographic territory, interestingly, is not necessarily a criterion for
identifying a people. If we think about how many ethnic conflicts, sometimes
dramatic and bloody, arise from disputes relating to land claims and occupa-
tion, it should be clear that belonging to a given territory is not an exclusive
right. In fact, several peoples or ethnic groups may have their roots in the
same region or portion of the world. Our all being siblings means establishing relationships of peaceful coexistence among peoples, among different
identities and cultures. Choosing peace, in fact, "is not to opt for a kind of
syncretism, or for the absorption of one into the other, but rather for a reso-

notion of "people" appears as an "open" category, in the sense that it refers to the life of human beings and to the possibility of giving rise to "a new synthesis" (*FT* 160) in which what is at first perceived as different and foreign is included and integrated, leading to the overcoming of inequities or unfairness.

Consequently, the adjective *popular* avoids every possible abstraction, since it refers to what is concretely linked to the identity of a "people-nation,"[7] and opens up a viable alternative for politics: the lived experience of each people stands between liberal individualism and xenophobic populism. Such experience consists of intermediate communities of persons who share common projects, dreams, desires for growth, and moments of concrete solidarity.

Pope Francis asks about the problem of work, since it is the means of guaranteeing a decent life and of ensuring co-responsibility in increasing social well-being. He points to work as the primary objective of "good politics." Since work represents an "essential dimension of social life" (*FT* 162), the best way to help those who find themselves disadvantaged is to allow them scope for initiative, access to the market, and the chance to use their own skills and resources.

Thus, the adjective *popular* is explained in the light of the complex reality of work, since the greatest form of social inequality consists in being deprived of the means that are indispensable to develop one's own potential. This is why the

---

lution which takes place on a higher plane and preserves what is valid and useful on both sides" (*EG* 228).

[7] Each people-nation is defined by a common culture, which is always the result of and rooted in a common history, but which also points forward toward a shared common good. Keep in mind that for Francis, the "poor and simple" are the stewards of the historical memory and cultural identity of a people (cf. *EN* 48; *EG* 124). Their aspirations toward justice are often expressed in manifestations of popular piety. This is the "popular wisdom" to which Pope Francis often alludes in his speeches and that he considers "the starting point for healing and liberation" from what threatens the fabric of society (cf. *EG* 68–69; 126).

concept of "people" finds strong resistance from neo-liberal economic viewpoints, whose theoretical presuppositions are anchored in individualism and therefore in a conception of society as "merely the sum of coexisting interests" (*FT* 163). Francis's critique of the "technocratic paradigm" (*FT* 166) is not limited to denouncing its erroneous conceptual framework or pointing out its detrimental effects, but it also confronts its concupiscent or "grasping" nature; the innate tendency to close in on oneself egotistically seems opposed to any possible imagining of social coexistence in which charity becomes the driving force behind "an effective process of historical change that embraces everything" (*FT* 164).

Politics today is marked by a loss of the "sense of responsibility" (*LS* 25) and by the illusion that technology will be able to fix everything (*LS* 109). By calling our concupiscent attitudes into question, the pope points the finger at the idolatry of money and its trappings and devices. Neo-liberalism is not only a theory but also presents itself as a creed. Its dogmatic structure is revealed when it postulates that the market is capable of resolving crises through its own laws and rules, or when it invokes "the magic theories of 'spillover' or 'trickle'" (*FT* 168) as the panacea for all social disparities.

But technical solutions are doomed to fail if social life is not reenvisioned in such a way as to reground its values, its ends, its means. If the economy is not rethought on the basis of concrete proposals of solidarity, then every solution for poverty is destined to prove incapable of changing the social order and the status quo.

The crisis unleashed by the COVID-19 pandemic has shown the above speculations to be illusory, since the free market has proven incapable of offering solutions at the global level. Rather, the pandemic has manifested all the weakness of political strategies that are based on economic theories and not on the recognition of human dignity. The pandemic represents an "event" from which any good politics should emerge changed, showing itself capable of making choices that do not exclusively follow the dictates of the market or respond only to the frenetic expectations of efficiency, but which place the value of the person at the center (*FT* 168).

Similarly, we see the importance of popular movements that give rise to alternative forms of economy and of community production. These movements go beyond the idea of "a policy *for* the poor" to a policy "*with* the poor" and "*of* the poor" (*FT* 169), in order to allow them to become protagonists and actors in social transformation.[8] When charity and trust become part of economic practice, it becomes possible to abandon a certain propensity for top-down social welfare policies. Instead, experiences that come together "from below" can flourish and generate creative forms of popular economy.

Charity as the "soul" of politics:
Acting on the global level

Rather than redistributing wealth, we should think about "the effective distribution of power (especially political, economic, defense-related, and technological power)" (*FT* 171). How good it would be to establish an international body governed by law and empowered to sanction those who use economic means to establish hidden forms of neo-colonialism. Likewise, how good it would be to establish international organizations with the authority to assure the common good on a global level and to work toward the achievement of pressing goals, such as the eradication of hunger, the end of human trafficking, and the protection of the environment.

There is also an urgent need to rethink the United Nations, broadening the bases for participation in order to prevent economically advanced nations from appropriating all the authority

---

[8] M. Czerny and P. Foglizzo, "The Strength of the Excluded: World Meeting of Popular Movements at the Vatican," in *Thinking Faith* (online journal of the Jesuits in Britain), January 29, 2015; and "The World Can Be Seen More Clearly from the Peripheries," in *Thinking Faith,* 2022.

(*FT* 173).[9] Politics must show itself capable of embracing a broad vision, promoting multilateralism (*FT* 144), strengthening the means for peacefully resolving conflicts (*FT* 174), rethinking the legal systems on the basis of international cooperation, and identifying objectives that go beyond a particular people's own interests (*FT* 177).

To the lack of coordination and various other deficiencies in the international community, Pope Francis positively contrasts the action of so many groups and organizations in civil society that put the principle of subsidiarity into practice in new ways. This offers some security to entire populations in precarious conditions. There is something heroic in their attempt to defend human rights from abusive customs and mentalities—often exacerbated by giving the economy priority over politics. Here is a reason to be hopeful for the future of our humanity.

Meanwhile an economy without politics is incapable of overcoming the crises; politics that merely submits to the dictates of the economy is blind. Both have to commit themselves, through mutual agreement, to developing an integral approach and to seeking good practices, combating corruption, the misuse of power, and failure to comply with the law. Planning together is to look toward the future, inspired jointly to pursue the common good. For it is a duty of justice to consider seriously the legacy that we will leave in the hands of future generations (*FT* 178).

Pope Francis reiterates that politics fulfills its own vocation when it pursues the common good. He adds that the political aspiration to good governance of the social order should impel

---

[9] In *Sollicitudo Rei Socialis*, John Paul II affirms that today humanity faces "a new and more difficult phase of its genuine development. It needs a greater degree of international ordering, at the service of the societies, economies and cultures of the whole world" (*SrS* 43). On the rethinking of the United Nations Organization, see John Paul II, *Address to the 50th General Assembly of the United Nations*, October 5, 1995, 14.

it to seek charity as the "soul" (*FT* 180) of its way of proceeding (*modus operandi*).

If "'person' and 'people' are correlative terms" (*FT* 182), "social love"[10] and "political charity"[11] are two sides of the same coin. At an interpersonal level, promoting the other and commitment to build a better society correspond with what politics accomplishes in the civil order. Through its inherent closeness to the truth, charity avoids sensationalism, the emotional wavelength, and always suggests a universal openness to problems. Social love is the surest way to achieve the development of everyone, because it is always creative and capable of opening up a path forward even where there seems to be no way out of the problems (*FT* 183). Moreover, social love enables

---

[10] The notion of "social love" is borrowed from *Redemptor Hominis* (*RH* 15). This passage from John Paul II's encyclical analyzes technological and scientific progress as a "sign of the times" that characterizes our era. John Paul II emphasizes the ambivalent nature of this kind of progress: it is an expression of human genius, yet it can become a threat with catastrophic consequences to the extent that it is seen as an end in itself. In order to avoid the perilous self-destruction of the human race, we must ask ourselves about the real advantages of techno-scientific progress. The criterion for this discernment is precisely that of social love. Does techno-scientific progress benefit everyone? Does it make human life "more human"? Or does it become a weapon in the hands of a select few in order to dominate others without regard for the possible consequences of its use? Cf. G. Tanzella-Nitti, "Pensare la tecnologia in prospettiva teologica: esiste un umanesimo scientifico?" in *Scienza, tecnologia e valori morali: quale futuro? Studi in onore di Francesco Barone*, ed. P. Barrotta G. O. Longo, and M. Negrottim Armando Editore, Roma 2011, 201–220; 155.

[11] In the Encyclical *Caritas in Veritate*, Benedict XVI took up the expression "political charity" in connection with the novel concept of "the institutional path of charity": "Every Christian is called to practice this charity, in a manner corresponding to his vocation and according to the degree of influence he wields in the *pólis*. This is the institutional path—we might also call it the political path—of charity, no less excellent and effective than the kind of charity which encounters the neighbor directly, outside the institutional mediation of the *pólis*" (*CiV* 7).

passing from personal initiative to joint action (*FT* 185). Politics that is animated by charity manages to become "universal" and to spread throughout the social fabric. The example used to illustrate charity in politics is enlightening: "If someone helps an elderly person cross a river, that is a fine act of charity. The politician, on the other hand, builds a bridge, and that too is an act of charity" (*FT* 186).

In the last part of chapter 5, Francis addresses politicians directly in a heartfelt appeal to their consciences. He tells them that overcoming the challenges of poverty and exclusion, eliminating hunger, and guaranteeing everyone the inalienable right to food (*FT* 189) are only possible by personally committing oneself, "rolling up one's sleeves," and honoring a preferential option for the poor that discourages any kind of "soulless pragmatism" (*FT* 187). This requires respect for each individual and the firm conviction of the prior inherent dignity of every person (*FT* 191). Politics must foster a diverse society and protect the variety of "voices" that make it up (*FT* 190). To this end, it is necessary to spread a culture of tolerance and peaceful coexistence. To offer attention and care to the little ones, to the weak and on the margins, is to allow oneself to "become tender" and touched in the depths by their dramatic experiences. Being sensitive to the injuries of others is not a sign of weakness but of immense inner strength (*FT* 194). Engaging in politics, not in order to amass power for oneself but with the goal of human promotion, is a way of sowing hope. When we truly desire to improve the living conditions of others, we are willing to intervene without worrying about immediate results, trusting that others will one day reap the benefits (*FT* 196). From this perspective, governing is a way of serving that opens up to the mystery of fruitfulness. When we forget about the image to project outward, about polls and public opinion, we are able to focus only on the good that can be done, initiating processes of change and transformation that are rooted in the present in order to nourish trust in the future (*FT* 197).

Dialogue and social friendship:
Approaching the other with respect in order
to seek the truth together

In recent decades, theological reflection has rediscovered the importance of dialogue for a more mature and complete expression of faith.[12] Vatican II already laid the groundwork for such a development by emphasizing the significance of "dialogue" for understanding the salvation-history event of divine Revelation. Indeed, the Dogmatic Constitution *Dei Verbum* recognizes "dialogue" as a fundamental theological category when it affirms that "God, out of the abundance of His love, speaks to men as friends and lives among them, so that He may invite and take them into fellowship with Himself" (*DV* 2).

Paul VI also attributed special importance to dialogue, identifying the term as the most suitable means of expressing the Church's renewed awareness of how to become present in the world. Instituted by Christ as an intrinsically *dialogical* reality, the Church is sent to proclaim the Gospel to all peoples. In the Encyclical *Ecclesiam Suam*, Pope Paul stated that it is precisely on the basis of *dialogue* that one can define the *mission* of the Church in today's world and, consequently, the two terms are so closely related that they can be understood as synonymous:

> If, as We said, the Church realizes what is God's will in its regard, it will gain for itself a great store of energy, and in addition will conceive the need for pouring out this energy

---

[12] The implications of a dialogical way of thinking have mostly been explored in the field of trinitarian theology, not only for the sake of a correct hermeneutics of the christological form of Revelation, but also in the face of current pastoral issues in the Church and ethical issues in society. From the truth of the One and triune God, in which otherness is the fruit of substantial love, "dialogue" emerges as a spiritual, cultural, and social event that is capable of developing an anthropology that is in turn dialogical. Cf. L. Sandonà, *Dialogica: per un pensare teologico tra sintassi trinitaria e questione del pratico,* Città Nuova, Roma 2019.

in the service of all men. It will have a clear awareness of a mission received from God, of a message to be spread far and wide. Here lies the source of our evangelical duty, our mandate to teach all nations. . . . To this internal drive of charity which seeks expression in the external gift of charity, we will apply the word "dialogue." The Church must enter into dialogue with the world in which it lives. It has something to say, a message to give, a communication to make. (*ES* 64–65)

Based on the teachings of Vatican II and Paul VI, it is clear that dialogue not only is a fundamental dimension of human and Christian experience, but also constitutes a special charism to help the Church in its commitment to promoting unity among peoples and our all being siblings.[13]

Nevertheless, even with this reappropriation of the "dialogue approach" in Church contexts, it is not unusual for those who favor dialogue as important in political, economic, and social choices, or in civil coexistence, to be reproached as naive dreamers. It is almost as if the very fact of approaching today's challenges by proposing and promoting an approach of dialogue betrays a sort of "doing good deeds" and "peacemaking" that are totally inadequate for grasping human reality and contemporary phenomena.

This prejudice is probably due to the way in which the meaning of dialogue has been misunderstood in the past, reducing it to a last resort when all else has failed. Only when everything seems to be irretrievably lost (*in extremis*), when no solution can possibly be found, does attempting the dialogue approach emerge as a means of damage control and of "salvaging whatever can still be saved."

Fratelli Tutti takes a different approach, speaking of dialogue with healthy and realistic proposals. Rather than being a last

---

[13] Cf. P. Rossano, "Il concetto e i presupposti del dialogo," in P. Roassano, *Dialogo e annuncio cristiano. L'incontro con le grandi religioni*, Edizioni Paoline, Cinisello Balsamo 1993, 13–26.

resort, an attempt to repair the damage and try to reconcile the parties, dialogue is proposed as a generative and "preventive" process that can open up horizons that go well beyond mere compromise. Far from being only an emergency "escape hatch," dialogue affects the parties involved, pushing them to review their own priorities and to identify an alternative path toward a sustainable future. Reducing the value of dialogue to a mere "remedy" diminishes its full power and effectiveness.[14]

Dialogue is an indispensable tool for bringing various social actors together and a point of encounter for diverse cultural identities (*FT* 199). The absence of dialogue always has harmful consequences, worsening the internal conflicts within a nation, for example, and exacerbating tensions among peoples (*FT* 202).

Pope Francis's vision of dialogue is not driven by the sole objective of explicitly proclaiming the Gospel. Rather, the pope's perspective follows the logic that Jesus revealed in the parable of the leaven in the dough (Mt 13:33). Dialogue aims to give rise from within to the interweaving of relationships and relations between persons and peoples. As Saint Paul VI affirmed, the person of dialogue's "constant endeavor is to get everyone talking about the message which it has been given to him to communicate" (*ES* 80). In other words, it is about enriching our grammar as human beings with the syntax of dialogue that Christ revealed to the world as he showed it the face of the Father.[15]

It is the encounter between the eternal *Logos* and human logic that shows us, above all, what dialogue is not. Dialogue is often confused with a frantic "bartering" of opinions, devoid of any sincere desire to understand the deeper reasons and intentions of the other. In that misunderstanding of dialogue,

---

[14] Cf. A. Fabris, *RelAzione. Una filosofia performativa,* Morcelliana, Brescia 2016, 175–180.

[15] Cf. P. Coda, "Nella logica del Dio unico che è Trinità," in *Dialogo dunque sono: come prendersi cura del mondo,* ed. L. Becchetti, P. Coda, and L. Sandonà, Città Nuova, Roma 2019, 45–63.

listening is not experienced as constructive, a way in which to open oneself to the truth of the interlocutor. Rather, listening is reduced to searching the words uttered by the opponent in order to find ammunition to make one's own argument more convincing. The systematic refusal to listen to the logic of others hardens our own positions and locks the dialogue into a stalemate.

The media teems with these kinds of fruitless exchanges of opinions, which masquerade as dialogue. In reality, they are overlapping monologues in the presence of the other side. This style has become prevalent not only on the internet, where aggression and hatred hide behind the impersonal communication offered by social media, but also in political debate, where the ability to prevail over one's opponent has become more important than the ideas that want expression.

Politicians have resorted to aggressive tones, derogatory language, and the manipulation of information, often in order to justify their choices, even at the cost of demonizing those who think differently than they do (*FT* 201). When the willingness to engage in dialogue is lacking, confrontation deteriorates into a conflict between opposing factions and interests and aims only at gaining the advantage. The best one can hope for is to reach an agreement on sharing the power, avoiding as much as possible that the others get "the biggest slice."

In order to build together, we need to learn the art of dialogue. This means welcoming the other's points of view and striving to understand the other's positions, without precluding from the start the possibility of finding something good or sensible. Tolerance emerges from the assiduous exercise of comparing diverse ideas, recognizing difference as an asset to safeguard and not to oppose. For this, it is fundamental to cultivate respect. There is no true dialogue if one is not willing to offer others due consideration, legitimating their identity and their different way of reasoning and living (*FT* 203). Differences can elicit primal emotions in us, triggering resistance and rejection and particular defense mechanisms: to "negate" the other or to relish the opportunity to oppose the other and or with cynical pleasure to exclude and ostracize.[16] Beginning in the 1990s, the problem of relativism found its way into many of the documents of John Paul II's Magisterium, especially regarding ethical questions. Benedict XVI further emphasized the need to demonstrate the theoretical and practical deficiencies of relativism in a more systematic way, in order to indicate an alternative path for the Christian faith. Benedict XVI treated relativism as a single phenomenon, without specifying its various manifestations or using adjectives to describe it (e.g., cultural, moral, ethical, religious, political). In a message addressed to young people, Benedict explained the harmful effects of relativism as follows: "There is a growing mentality of relativism, which holds that everything is equally valid, that truth and absolute points of reference do not exist. But this way of thinking does not lead to true freedom, but rather to instability, confusion and blind conformity to the fads of the moment." Thus, the critique of relativism is seen as part of the dialectic with secularized society, which is framed in relation to the removal of the metaphysical, ethical, spiritual, and eschatological dimensions that accompanied the advent of modernity.

Dialogue keeps us from falling into simplistic generalizations, for there is no one way of seeing reality and finding its meaning. Today, for example, we run this risk when we think that scientific progress is the only meaningful and reliable narrative for today's world. An integral approach to life, however, requires that the various sciences interact with one another, sharing the lessons that each perspective on reality can offer to the other disciplines (*FT* 204). For a long time, the fragmentation of knowledge was supported by relativism,[17] and

---

[16] Cf. M. Aime, *Una bella differenza. Alla scoperta della diversità del mondo,* Einaudi, Torino 2016.

[17] Cf. Benedict XVI, *Message for the XXVI World Youth Day (2011),* August 6, 2010; cf. J. Ratzinger, "Salvezza e storia," in *Storia e dogma,* Jaca Book, Milano 1971, 93–110; cf. J. Ratzinger, "Ragione e fede. Scambio reciproco per un'etica comune," in J. Habermas, *Ragione e fede in dialogo,* ed.

in the name of mutual tolerance, objective truth or universally valid principles were denied. However, no real advantage has been gained from this approach, which has only weakened our knowledge and built up "Cartesian walls" that have ended up isolating various fields of research and disconnecting them from one another (*FT* 206). We must recognize that while facts can in their interpretation be misunderstood or intentionally tampered with, there are truths that do not change and that transcend time (*FT* 208). Contrary to what is commonly asserted, human reason is not "weak," but has the necessary strength within itself to discover these universal principles and immutable values to which it is naturally disposed. One of these fundamental and inalienable truths is the dignity of the human person (*FT* 207), which shields human beings from the convictions that arbitrarily ebb and flow throughout history. The same truth frees humanity from fleeting fashions and persuasive ideologies that threaten to bend and break the human according to certain agendas and interests. Relativism includes the risk that the strongest will impose what is to be held as true and that justice will simply mirror dominant ideas (*FT* 210). In contrast, basic morality affirms the existence of laws and norms that are valid for all human beings, apart from any kind of contingencies. "It makes no difference whether one is the master of the world or the 'poorest of the poor' on the face of the earth. Before the demands of morality we are all absolutely equal" (*FT* 209). This means seeking the truth together, knowing it in its real objectivity, going beyond "any ephemeral consensus" (*FT* 211), and overcoming every kind of political appropriation of the truth that limits it to a single point of view (*FT* 206).

Promoting a healthy "culture of encounter" is the prerequisite for achieving a social compact in which no one is denied rights and opportunities (*FT* 215–221). Pope Francis recommends

---

G. Bosetti, Marsilio, Venezia 2005, 65–81; cf. J. Ratzinger, "Fede, religione e cultura," in *Fede, Verità, Tolleranza. Il Cristianesimo e le religioni del mondo*, Edizioni Cantagalli, Siena 2003, 57–82; cf. J. Ratzinger, "Relativismo, problema della fede," in *Il Regno-Documenti* 784, no. 1 (1997): 51–56.

kindness as an attitude of respect and as a resolution not to hurt others (*FT* 223). Exchanging with one another, without relativizing one's own opinions or those of the other, is the most immediate way to transform social relationships and lay the foundation for a harmonious coexistence that is fruitful for all (*FT* 224).

Pathways toward a new encounter: Builders and artisans of peace

Chapter 7 of *Fratelli Tutti* addresses the problem of peace and of the great changes to the management of international conflicts brought about by the advent of globalization and techno-scientific progress.

It is worth remembering that until the second half of the twentieth century, the Magisterium of the Church showed little interest in the question of peace. It was only after the Second World War, in the face of the wounds inflicted upon humanity by the war, that the Magisterium felt the need to study the topic more deeply.[18]

The Encyclical *Pacem in Terris* of John XXIII and the Pastoral Constitution *Gaudium et Spes* bear the most authoritative witness to the significant development that took place in the Church's theological consciousness on the topic of peace in the aftermath of World War II. Peace was no longer considered solely as the eschatological goal of the final recapitulation in Christ, but as a reality within history and as a task that the human family is called to accomplish here and now in the present.[19]

---

[18] The theme of peace was originally treated as a moral issue, either in response to the question of the legitimacy of war, or as part of the dogmatic reflection on the ultimate things, namely, death, judgment, hell, and heaven. Cf. E. Chiavacci, "Pace," in *Teologia*, ed. G. Barbaglio, G. Bof, S. Dianich, Edizioni San Paolo, Cinisello Balsamo 2002, 1048–1064, 164.

[19] Cf. J. Joblin, "L'actualité de l'enseignement de Gaudium et spes sur la paix," in *La pace: sfida all'Università Cattolica, Atti del Simposio fra le Università ecclesiastiche e gli Istituti di Studi Superiori di Roma, Roma*

In the light of the Council's teaching and the renewed sensitivity of the Magisterium, *Fratelli Tutti* sees peacemaking as a duty to proclaim the Gospel and to carry out God's plan for humanity in a way that is not yet *definitive*, but very much *real* as we strive constantly toward the final goal. The history of humanity and the history of salvation are not incommensurable; the former is an integral part of the latter. *Gaudium et Spes* speaks of peace in chapter V of Part II. However, the foundation of a theology of peace is found in Part I, specifically in the affirmation that "the Lord is the goal of human history" (*GS* 45). In contrast to any private notion of peace, *Gaudium et Spes* explains that peace is a responsibility that belongs to the entire human family, called to become the "family of God" (*GS* 40). Pope Francis's invitation to *all being siblings* is founded on this conviction: all of humanity must direct history toward the realization of peace. This objective is for everyone, though it acquires a particular importance for Christians, since it means showing the world the saving work of Christ.

Pope Francis indicates two different levels for carrying out our commitment to peace. There is a *political* level, which is the prerogative of institutions as they work through the art of negotiation. Then there is the *personal* level, which is every person of good will offering his or her contribution in order to increase the culture of peaceful social coexistence. Peace is the result of concerted efforts at both levels, since peace treaties—though indispensable—cannot achieve their goal without the contribution of civil communities and without the transformation of social relations that occurs through the direct and daily involvement of ordinary people.[20] Peace presupposes

---

(3–6 Dicembre 1986), ed. F. Biffi, Herder-FIUC, Roma 1988, 596–599; cf. M. Dagras, "La dynamique de l'encyclique," in *Paix sur la terre. Actualité d'une encyclique*, ed. R. Coste, M. Dagras, and G. Mathon, Centurion, Paris 1992, 19–38.

[20] Paul VI outlined the importance of personally and collectively contributing to the building of peace in civil society: "If public opinion is the element that determines the fate of the Peoples, the fate of Peace also depends on each of us. For each of us forms part of the civic body operating with a democratic system, which, in varying forms and degrees, today characterizes

that these two interrelated agencies—the political and the personal—converge to accomplish the common goal of together building a future without war.

To paraphrase a famous maxim of Tertullian's,[21] we can affirm that "peacemakers are not born, but become so." This is because building a peaceful world is the result of a journey of conversion that works at various levels to discipline our innate human tendency to overpower the weaker. This *becoming*, like Tertullian's, is where to find an "asceticism" or discipline that is oriented toward peace among religions, nations, and people.

While politics develops an "architecture" of peace, striving to assemble normative frameworks and build up international agreements, the web of peaceful relationships is woven by ordinary people and constitutes a "craftsmanship or handicraft" of peace (*FT* 231).

By resorting to these two images—"architecture" and "craftsmanship"—with the latter going back to the applied arts, Pope Francis articulates the theme of peace and proposes its future pathway in a way that resonates with "theological aesthetics." To build peace is *philokalia*, that is, loving and walking a path of beauty.[22] Peace is *beautiful* because it contrasts the

---

the life of the Nations organized in a modern manner. This is what we wished to say: Peace is possible, if each one of us wants it; if each one of us loves Peace, educates and forms his own outlook to Peace, defends Peace, works for Peace. Each one of us must listen in his own conscience to the impelling call: '*Peace depends on you too.*'" Paul VI, "Peace Depends on You Too," *Message for the Celebration of the VII Day of Peace*, January 1, 1974.

[21] Cf. Tertullian, *Apology*, *Ante-Nicene Fathers*, vol. 3., trans. S. Thelwall, ed. A. Roberts, J. Donaldson, and A. Cleveland Coxe (Buffalo, NY: Christian Literature Publishing Co., 1885), XVIII.

[22] Asceticism, from the Greek verb *áskēin*—meaning "to practice" or "to exercise"—signifies repeated action in an effort to acquire a skill. In ancient Greek literature this verb was used to indicate artistic work; asceticism is the effort needed so that the beautiful can take shape. The choice of the terms "architecture" and "craftsmanship" to indicate the effort of building a peaceful world points to an asceticism of peace, in which the effort made in the present is oriented toward giving future generations a truer, better, and more beautiful world. Cf. E. Bianchi, *Lessico della vita interiore. Le parole della spiritualità,* Rizzoli, Milano 2004.

ugliness of egoism and individualism and is the fruit of a common effort that needs commitment and dedication.[23] In the light of the Christian faith, peace is not the product of a heroic effort on the part of the individual, but an event of communion. Peace is a reflection of the "circular life" (*perichoresis*) of the Trinity, the interwoven agape of the Father, Son, and Holy Spirit. This trinitarian love is not only at the origin of the act of creation, but also constitutes its ultimate goal. Peace is the prophecy of a redeemed world, an anticipation of humanity reunited in the heavenly Jerusalem. At the same time, peace is a "sign of the times" that speaks of the presence of the Kingdom of God already at work in contemporary history, since it bears witness to the salvation unfolding in our history.

Pope Francis distills three qualities from biblical revelation that describe peace as the creation of a communal style that involves the human person in relationship with God, with creation, and with fellow human beings: truth, justice, and forgiveness.[24] The absence of any one of these attributes

---

[23] If beauty is an experience of a special resonance with creation and our fellow human beings, in which—as Hans Urs von Balthasar would say—we are given the possibility of perceiving the christological form, and which has the effect of expanding and extending our inner world, then peace is beautiful because it allows us to conquer parts of ourselves that can only be expressed in living out our profound interconnectedness in a way that is devoid of selfish and violent impulses toward others. Cf. C. Barone, "'L'esistenza dei Santi è teologia vissuta': Dogmatica e Spiritualità nell'apologetica teologica di Hans Urs von Balthasar," in *Synaxis* 37, no. 2 (2019): 133–153.

[24] In the Old Testament, peace (*shalom*) is blessing, rest, glory, wealth, and life. In other words, peace expresses a reality that the people of Israel already experience and witness in history, but whose full realization is the object of eschatological hope (Ex 57:19–21). The relationship that God establishes with the Chosen People constitutes a covenant of peace (Ez 37:26). It is often associated with the fulfillment of God's plan of salvation as *justice* (Ex 32:16–18; Lev 26:1–13; Prov 12:20) and as *truth* about the person (Ps 84:11–12). Since sin hinders the establishment of the Kingdom of God (Jer 6:13–14), Israel experiences peace as the *forgiveness* of sins and reconciliation with God. In the New Testament, peace (*eirènè*) is the personal gift of the Risen Lord to the community of believers (Lk 24:36; Jn 20:19, 21, 26), which was promised by Jesus during the time of his public ministry as a beatitude for those

undermines the very meaning of peace and the sense of *wholeness* to which it strives in social relations and throughout the world.[25] Truth, justice, and mercy are co-essential to peace, and each of them "prevents the other from being altered" (*FT* 227).[26]

To begin with the "stark and clear" truth (*FT* 226) means initiating processes that restore and heal the injuries caused by conflicts and wars (*FT* 225). These paths always imply the exercise of "a penitential memory, one that can accept the past in order not to cloud the future" (*FT* 226).[27] Only on the basis of historical truth, from an honest examination of the facts, can there be mutual understanding and a commitment to the common good that is open to the search for real solutions and new

---

who believe in him (Lk 10:5f.). In the letters of Saint Paul, peace is Christ himself (Eph 2:14–18), as salvation that is achieved through reconciliation with the Father, which happens through justification by faith (Rom 5:1). Cf. J.-Y. Lacoste, "Pace," in J.-Y. Lacoste, *Dizionario Critico di Teologia*, ed. P. Coda, Borla/Città Nuova, Roma 2005, 958–960; cf. G. Barbaglio, *Pace e violenza nella Bibbia*, Edizioni Dehoniane, Bologna 2011.

[25] The Hebrew word *shalom* comes from a root that designates the fact of being intact, complete (Heb 9:4). It alludes to the completion of a task, such as the construction of a house (1 Kgs 9:25), or the fact of restoring a reality to its condition of primordial integrity, such as paying off a creditor's debt (Ex 21:34) or fulfilling a vow (Ps 50:14). Therefore, biblical peace is not only the effect of a treaty or a "pact" that puts an end to a "time of war" (Eccl 3:8; Rev 6:3). Rather, biblical peace indicates the state of daily well-being that human beings derive from living in harmony with self, with God, and with others. Cf. X. Léon-Dufour, "Pace," in *Dizionario di Teologia Biblica*, Marietti, Genova 1995, 814–822.

[26] Cardinal Martini demonstrated how truth, justice, and forgiveness have been presented as co-essential elements of peace in the papal Magisterium following the Second Vatican Council, especially through the annual messages for the World Day of Peace. Cf. C. M. Martini, "Pace," in *Dizionario di Dottrina Sociale della Chiesa. Scienze sociali e Magistero*, Vita e Pensiero, Milano 2004, 94–107.

[27] On the need to purify our memory through forgiveness and reconciliation in order to reread the facts of the past through a new lens, see John Paul II, "Dialogue between Cultures for a Civilization of Love and Peace," *Message for the XXXIV World Day of Peace,* January 1, 2001, 21.

syntheses.[28] It is a duty of justice, but also a right of victims, to bring to light the genesis of a conflict, explaining its causes and recounting what really happened. Shedding light on events, without omitting or manipulating any facts, and recognizing the mistakes made by each of the parties involved, is a way of honoring the fallen and healing the injuries of the past. Truth is an antidote to revenge and a deterrent to the hatred that breeds more hate.

Peace "is not merely the absence of war" (*FT* 233), but the establishment of relations of social friendship in which the dignity of the human person is recognized and guaranteed. For this reason, peace demands justice and calls for a preferential option for the poor.[29] Without fairness and the guarantee that the marginalized really be protagonists of their own life, no social peace can actually take hold (*FT* 234). Indeed, social disparities constitute a fertile breeding ground for the proliferation of wars (*FT* 235). What often causes social unrest is the lack of

---

[28] Saint John Paul II pointed to truth as the foundation of peace, affirming that in order to fight against evil in the world we must always clarify the facts: "It demands that truth be restored, in order to keep individuals, groups, and nations from losing confidence in peace and from consenting to new forms of violence." John Paul II, "Truth, the Power of Peace," *Message for the XIII World Day of Peace,* January 1, 1980, 3.

[29] The connection between peace and poverty was outlined by Pope John Paul II: "Our world also shows increasing evidence of *another grave threat to peace:* many individuals and indeed whole peoples are living today *in conditions of extreme poverty.* The gap between rich and poor has become more marked, even in the most economically developed nations. *This is a problem which the conscience of humanity cannot ignore,* since the conditions in which a great number of people are living are an insult to their innate dignity and as a result are a threat to the authentic and harmonious progress of the world community. The gravity of this situation is being felt in many countries of the world: in Europe as well as in Africa, Asia, and America. In various regions the social and economic challenges which believers and all people of good will have to face are many. Poverty and destitution, social differences and injustices, some of them even legalized, fratricidal conflicts and oppressive regimes—all of these appeal to the conscience of whole peoples in every part of the world." John Paul II, "If You Want Peace, Reach Out to the Poor," *Message for the XXVI World Day of Peace*, January 1, 1993, 1.

conditions needed to assure the "discarded" access to integral human development. This is often at the origin of many anti-social attitudes and the backdrop for feelings of frustration and rage that can trigger sudden and violent reactions.[30]

Pope Francis wonders what meaning we can give to the word *reconciliation* and notes that many people avoid using it because they are convinced that conflict is part and parcel of the functioning of society (*FT* 236). They prefer to maintain only a semblance of peace, even at the cost of concealing problems and tacitly endorsing the perpetration of injustice. They then take advantage of appearances to avoid giving up their positions of power or profit.[31]

---

[30] From a moral perspective, Saint Paul VI linked the theme of peace with that of human development in *Populorum Progressio*, to the point of affirming that development is the new name for peace (*PP* 76–87). For his part, Saint John Paul II, in *Sollicitudo Rei Socialis*, highlighted the importance of solidarity as "the path to peace and at the same time to development" (*SrS* 39). Referring to the teaching of his predecessors, Pope Francis reiterates that the innate and inviolable dignity of the human person is not only a firm foundation for the building of lasting peace, but is also the guiding principle that enables political choices to prevent instability, rebellion, and violence. Paul VI, "The Promotion of Human Rights, the Way to Peace," *Message for the II World Day of Peace*, January 1, 1969; John Paul II, "Respect for Human Rights: The Secret of True Peace," *Message for the XXXII World Day of Peace,* January 1, 1999.

[31] Regarding the rethinking of economic models and the imperative of combining the globalization of markets with solidarity, John Paul II affirmed: "For this to happen, a complete change of perspective will be needed: it is no longer the well-being of any one political, racial or cultural community that must prevail, but rather the good of humanity as a whole. The pursuit of the common good of a single political community cannot be in conflict with *the common good of humanity,* expressed in the recognition of and respect for human rights sanctioned by the Universal Declaration of Human Rights of 1948. It is necessary, then, to abandon ideas and practices—often determined by powerful economic interests—which subordinate every other value to the absolute claims of the nation and the State. In this new perspective, the political, cultural and institutional divisions and distinctions by which humanity is ordered and organized are legitimate in so far as they are compatible with membership in the one human family, and with the ethical and legal requirements which stem from this. . . . Perhaps the time has come for *a new and*

However, there are situations before which we cannot close our eyes, just as there are unavoidable conflicts. In both cases, it is necessary to take a stand. We must renounce the advantages that can flow from not getting involved and prioritize the choice to oppose any kind of oppression. True reconciliation does not shy away from conflict and confrontation but goes through it, drawing from dialogue the determination needed to overcome conflict in a transparent and irreproachable way (*FT* 244).

Initiating processes of reconciliation requires time and patience. It demands respect for the memory of victims and, without falling into a spiral of revenge, renouncing reprisals (*FT* 251). It is essential that the firm decision to oppose injustice not be motivated by hatred or the desire for revenge.[32] Nor should it give rise to retribution with the hope of gaining some reparation (*FT* 242; 252). Peace is achieved by overcoming evil with good, for the true demonstration of strength lies in renouncing revenge (*FT* 243; 251).

---

deeper reflection on the nature of the economy and its purposes. What seems to be urgently needed is a reconsideration of the concept of 'prosperity' itself, to prevent it from being enclosed in a narrow utilitarian perspective which leaves very little space for values such as solidarity and altruism." John Paul II, "Peace on Earth to Those Whom God Loves!" *Message for the XXXIII World Day of Peace*, January 1, 2000, 6; 15.

[32] John Paul II indicated that forgiveness is an essential condition for the exercise of justice that is oriented toward peace: "True peace therefore is the fruit of justice, that moral virtue and legal guarantee which ensures full respect for rights and responsibilities, and the just distribution of benefits and burdens. But because human justice is always fragile and imperfect, subject as it is to the limitations and egoism of individuals and groups, it must include and, as it were, be completed by the *forgiveness that heals and rebuilds troubled human relations from their foundations*. This is true in circumstances great and small, at the personal level or on a wider, even international scale. Forgiveness is in no way opposed to justice, as if to forgive meant to overlook the need to right the wrong done. It is rather the fullness of justice, leading to that tranquility of order which is much more than a fragile and temporary cessation of hostilities, involving as it does the deepest healing of the wounds that fester in human hearts. Justice and forgiveness are both essential to such healing." John Paul II, "No Peace without Justice, No Justice without Forgiveness," *Message for the XXXV World Day of Peace*, January 1, 2002, 3.

Recalling one of the four principles expressed in *Evangelii Gaudium*, Pope Francis reaffirms that "unity is greater than conflict" (*EG* 228). At the same time, forgiveness is always a deeply personal matter and cannot be imposed from above. The goal of unity that leads to peace, to the resolution of conflicts, requires tolerance and calls for refraining from judging those who struggle to find the path of forgiveness (*FT* 246). In any case, seeking unity beyond conflict is never the same as forgetting; it does not mean erasing or denying the past (*FT* 250). On the contrary, the horrors committed by humanity, such as the Holocaust or the atomic bombs dropped on Hiroshima and Nagasaki (*FT* 247–248), must remain alive in our collective historical memory. New generations must not be allowed to grow up ignorant or indifferent to what happened to the victims of global conflicts. It would be a grave error to anesthetize our memory and distance ourselves from the events triggered by human evil. To avoid repeating the tragedies of the past, it is necessary to safeguard our collective consciousness, keeping it awake and ready to react to the will to dominate and overpower (*FT* 249).

Alongside the memories of the past that make us ashamed of the violence committed by people against their fellow human beings, we also need to hand down the testimony of those who, managing to go beyond the evil they have suffered, recover their dignity and keep on forgiving, showing solidarity, and acting as siblings. If forgiveness is to be received in the light of the mystery of God, as a real expression of divine love, then it is possible to forgive even someone who shows no signs of repentance or is reluctant to ask for forgiveness (*FT* 250). Forgiveness is a responsible choice; it includes the determination to break the vicious circle of revenge, firmly convinced that inflicting further suffering on those responsible for past crimes does not repair the damage done to their victims (*FT* 251). This does not mean that they should go unpunished, but only that justice should be exercised out of love for justice, and not as a means of giving free rein to rage (*FT* 252).

Two "false answers": War and the death penalty

Peace must always be achieved through the full protection of life and the firm condemnation of every form of revenge, such as war and the death penalty, that negates life's inherent value. These two are really "false answers" (*FT* 255) to the problems they claim to solve. Their only effect is to generate new tensions and to tear apart the social fabric even further.

As far as war is concerned, it is a mirage to think it could be a valid response to the onset of conflict. Most often, criminal intentions and sordid ulterior motives, such as ambitions to dominate, abuses of power, and racial prejudice, lurk behind the apparent reasons invoked to justify war as an effective or unavoidable option (*FT* 256). Pope Francis highlights the harmful consequences that inevitably follow the choice of war: "war is the negation of all rights and a dramatic assault on the environment" (*FT* 257). Thus, war is an existential risk that should be avoided at all costs because of the damage it causes to human development and to creation.

Historical evidence shows how the application of the Charter of the United Nations has proven, over the decades, to be an effective tool in the management of international crises. However, it cannot be denied that in certain circumstances the arbitrary decision not to apply its binding norms has served to mask particular interests, with considerable damage to the common good of the world. It is deplorable and narrow-minded to resort to war, citing humanitarian needs as an excuse, and to manipulate information in order to disguise the decision to be violent as legitimate.

There is no justification for war; nor is it ever licit to present it as a "just" solution,[33] as a preventive or defensive action, as

---

[33] As mentioned above, in theological reflection prior to the twentieth century the theme of peace was examined only in relation to the reality of war. While in the early days of Christianity the prohibition on killing was absolute, even against an unjust aggressor, a casuistic approach developed in the era of Constantine in which the possibility of a "just war" was seen as

if to elevate it to a plausible means of definitively settling disputes (*FT* 258). Faced with the possibility of causing suffering and death to entire populations, it is not permissible to appeal to the principle of "the lesser evil." This is all the more true in an era in which the military applications of technology have produced sophisticated weapons with unimaginable destructive power compared to the past.

Globalization, then, means that the conflicts that take place in a given part of the world produce a chain reaction with repercussions all over the planet. We are living in a "world war fought piecemeal" (*FT* 25; 259). It is naive to believe that what happens on another continent does not concern us or does not affect us directly. Every war must be "deeply felt" as a failure of politics and a defeat for humanity, because it "leaves our world worse than it was before" (*FT* 261). For this reason, it is important that the drama endured by civilians challenge us, connecting us with the pain of the victims, of refugees, of orphans, and of those mutilated in body and spirit, even if these are often considered an inevitable or collateral effect of the events they are caught up in. If it is true that "realities are

---

legitimate. For example, in the writings of Saints Ambrose and Augustine, war is seen as an instrument for the defense of peoples, while the biblical ideal of peace is increasingly perceived through an eschatological lens. The idea of war in order to promote Christianity also came to the fore, and it has been invoked many times over the centuries, for example, in the Crusades, in the evangelization of Europe, in the conquest of the Americas, and more recently in the armed struggle between Catholics and Protestants in Ireland or in the clash between Catholics and Orthodox in the Balkans. Officially, no war has been declared unjust by ecclesiastical authorities. Even Pope Benedict XV's ardent warnings against the onset of World War I described the impending conflict as "useless slaughter," but not necessarily unjust. In this light, Pope Francis's affirmations in *Fratelli Tutti* appear prophetic and innovative: "We can no longer think of war as a solution, because its risks will probably always be greater than its supposed benefits. In view of this, it is very difficult nowadays to invoke the rational criteria elaborated in earlier centuries to speak of the possibility of a 'just war.' Never again war!" (*FT* 258). Cf. C. Bresciani and L. Eusebi, *Ha ancora senso parlare di guerra giusta? Le recenti elaborazioni della teologia morale,* EDB, Bologna 2010.

greater than ideas" (*EG* 231–233), then the reality of war as undergone by the victims surpasses the idea of whoever considers it advantageous in the short or long term.

Francis urges the international community to undertake a serious and comprehensive reflection on how to respond correctly to the realities of evil that stand in the way of a peaceful world. This means to overcome all arguments that are essentially utilitarian and substantially bound to a retributive vision of justice that applies retaliation as a punitive and preventive measure.

If the response to a crime has the effect of damaging or denying the values and rights that the response is intended to preserve, then the end result will simply be to encourage the legitimization of violence in society.[34] Effective long-term prevention does not depend on counterproductive tactics of intimidation, such as threating sanctions or the use of nuclear weapons (*FT* 262). Rather, sustainable prevention relies on the legal system's ability to maintain in society a high level of social consensus and respect for legal norms. Nothing better upholds the authority of a law that has been violated than the fact that an offender recognizes the injustice that he or she has committed and embarks on taking responsibility for what was done. Using fear as a pedagogical device and trying to maintain international balances of power on the basis of deterrence have bred devastating phenomena, such as terrorism, and have undermined trust between peoples.

Hence, Pope Francis addresses this sensible and daring proposal to all countries: renounce nuclear power,[35] renounce weapons of mass destruction, and use the enormous amounts

---

[34] The essence of laws must be ordered to the common good. Legislators or legislative systems that are at odds with the fundamental interests of a community or of the human person lose de facto all validity: they are no longer law (*ius*); rather, they degenerate into abuse (*foeda iniuria*)—as Saint John XXIII strongly affirmed in *Pacem in Terris* 30.

[35] Following in the footsteps of his predecessors, Pope Francis has repeatedly pointed to the path of disarmament. During his apostolic journey to Japan, the pope reiterated: "With deep conviction I wish once more to declare that the use of atomic energy for purposes of war is today, more than ever, a crime not only against the dignity of human beings but against any possible

of money usually invested in the military sector to create a "global fund" to solve the problem of hunger and promote the development of the poorer countries (*FT* 262).

Thus, if we look to respond to evil consistently with good—admittedly, a demanding commitment—then this guiding principle must be extended not only to countries but also to criminal persons. In this sense, as Saint John Paul II already declared, the death penalty as a just or legal response to certain grave crimes that an individual can be guilty of should be considered "inadequate from a moral standpoint and no longer necessary from that of penal justice" (*FT* 263).

By citing scriptural passages and patristic texts (*FT* 264–265), *Fratelli Tutti* recovers a vision more consonant with the Christian message. The penalty imposed on someone who has committed heinous crimes must not obey a vindictive logic,[36] lending itself to fear and resentment, but must be conceived "as part of a process of healing and reintegration into society" (*FT* 266). Since not even those who are guilty of murder lose their inalienable dignity as human beings, even in these cases the punishment must seek a justice that heals and restores.[37]

---

future for our common home." Francis, *Address at the Meeting for Peace at the Peace Memorial in Hiroshima*, November 24, 2019.

[36] The relationship between Christian doctrine and criminal law has developed over the centuries on the basis of a glaring misunderstanding, namely, that of considering the model of retributive justice as conforming to the truth of the Gospel. This has led to a significant reciprocal conditioning. On the one hand, the penal practice of States has inflicted punishments according to retributive criteria that relied on presumed theological and religious presuppositions as a legitimizing cultural factor. On the other hand, theology has drawn elements from penal systems that have influenced its reflections on the juridical and moral fields. A more careful exegetical reading of biblical texts demonstrates that it is not possible to derive from them certain concepts of punishment that are based on an idea of retributive justice. Rather, the opposite is true, namely, that the retributive conception of justice has altered our perception of the authentic concept of justice that emerges from the Bible and from the entire event of Revelation. Cf. L. Eusebi, "Diritto penale," in *Dizionario di Dottrina Sociale della Chiesa*, 251–261.

[37] The theological interpretation of the mystery of Christ's death on the cross in a hamartia-centric lens focuses on human sin as the cause of the

Pope Francis reiterates what he already said about the death penalty in the rescript of 2018 approving a new version of no. 2267 of the *Catechism of the Catholic Church*: "the death penalty is inadmissible because it is an attack on the inviolability and dignity of the person."[38]

This change is a significant development of doctrine and refocuses its ethical position in favor of human life, in the light of the Gospel, and in continuity with the Magisterium of the twentieth-century popes.[39]

Incarnation, by means of the category of "satisfaction," "vicarious substitution," or "penal expiation"—as is the case in the work of Saint Anselm of Canterbury, *Cur deus homo*. For centuries, this sin-centered perspective conditioned the concept of punishment that was elaborated by the juridical-moral reflection of the Catholic Church, obscuring the perception of the very linchpin of the Christian faith. However, redemption is not accomplished because of the sufferings endured by Christ in order to appease an angry God and thus pay "the price" of human sin. Rather, redemption is won through the total offering of Christ as he gave himself to the Father in the totality of his earthly existence, as the Incarnate Word. It is not suffering in itself but rather charity that is reparatory, of which the death on the Cross is the utmost expression. Otherwise, we remain in a worldly juridical perspective, which would consider it licit to respond to evil with evil, attributing redemptive value to evil instead of love. The saving mystery of Jesus's death on the Cross reveals God's very being as love that is poured out unconditionally even in the face of human sin. Thus, God's justice is expressed in Jesus as the pouring out of love in the face of evil. Cf. N. Albanesi, *Cur deus homo: la logica della redenzione. Studio sulla teoria della soddisfazione di S. Anselmo arcivescovo di Canterbury*, PUG, 2002, 14–80; cf. *La teologia del XX secolo: un bilancio.2. Prospettive sistematiche*, G. Canobio—P. Coda, eds., Vol. 2, Città Nuova, Roma 2003, 64–72. 184.

[38] Cf. Francis, *New Revision of Number 2267 of the* Catechism of the Catholic Church *on the Death Penalty—Rescriptum "ex Audentia SS.mi,"* August 2, 2018.

[39] In the face of modern totalitarianism, Popes Pius XI and Pius XII affirmed the centrality and value of the human person. The Second Vatican Council confirms this position in *Gaudium et Spes* by declaring: "The beginning, the subject, and the goal of all social institutions is and must be the human person" (*GS* 25). This lays the foundation for objecting to the first traditional argument in favor of the death penalty, in which the offender was deemed to be a sick part of the social body and therefore liable to "surgery" or sacrifice should the good of the community be put at risk. This notion was

Indeed, the traditional teaching of the Church, succinctly expressed in the previous formulation of the *Catechism*, did not exclude recourse to the death penalty when this was the only viable way to effectively defend human lives from an unjust aggressor. However, assuming that the true identity and full responsibility of the guilty party had been ascertained, even the former *Catechism* text modified the legitimacy of applying the death penalty, observing that the conditions that could have once made it admissible are "practically non-existent" today.[40]

The crux of the matter is the way we define and interpret the notion of "legitimate self-defense," understood as an action opposing and proportionate to an aggressive behavior underway.[41] The penal intervention of the State has often been

---

based on a well-known passage of the *Summa Theologiae* of Saint Thomas Aquinas (*S.Th.*, II-II, q.64, a.2). Cardinal Luis Ladaria, SJ, prefect of the Congregation for the Doctrine of the Faith, commented that the *Catechism*'s new text regarding the death penalty "situates itself in continuity with the preceding Magisterium while bringing forth a coherent development of Catholic doctrine." We have come a long way: from the memorable text of the Social Commission of the French Bishops' Conference against the death penalty in 1978, to the teachings of all the recent popes. Suffice it to think, for example, of Benedict XVI's Exhortation *Africae Munus*, whose condemnation of the death penalty reflects the ecclesial conscience of faith matured in the light of Vatican II (*AM* 83). Cf. Congregation of the Doctrine of the Faith, *Letter to the Bishops regarding the New Revision of Number 2267 of the* Catechism of the Catholic Church *on the Death Penalty*, August 1, 2018, 7; cf. Benedict XVI, *Post-Synodal Apostolic Exhortation "Africae Munus,"* November 19, 2011, 83; cf. C. Dounot, "Une solution de continuité doctrinale. Peine de mort et enseignement de l'Église," in *Catholica* 141 (2018): 46–73.

[40] In 1997, the original edition of the *Catechism*, which had been first published five years prior, was revised to incorporate the words of John Paul II in *Evangelium Vitae* (no. 56), in which the pontiff affirmed the practical non-existence of the conditions that could theoretically legitimize recourse to the death penalty today.

[41] There are essentially three conditions for "legitimate self-defense." The first is expressed by the maxim *moderamen inculpatae tutelae*, i.e., provided that recourse to force is an extreme remedy. This means that nonviolent and less violent means of deterrence and defense must have been considered and tried first, and have proved impracticable or ineffective. The second condition is that the aggressor's violence be current and ongoing, not hypothetical,

framed in a "relative" perspective, in accordance with the contingent needs of safeguarding the common good. As a result, the concept of "legitimate self-defense" was absorbed by that of "social defense." The risk is an undue exercise of social defense based on what is traditionally allowed in the case of legitimate self-defense. This causes an overlapping between the concept of prevention and that of legitimate self-defense. Therefore, on the one hand, it can be deduced that "social defense" has never been applicable in practice, since court sentences are not a form of "legitimate self-defense." On the other hand, a space remained open for arguing a presumed inevitability, in certain cases, of recourse to the death penalty in order to defend society from crime. Francis notes how such positions are taken advantage of to endorse, in some countries and to this very day, the custom of resorting "to preventive custody, imprisonment without trial" (*FT* 266), or worse, to justify "extrajudicial or extralegal executions" (*FT* 267). Indeed, dictatorial and totalitarian regimes invoke the concept of "social defense" using the death penalty as a tool for suppressing political dissidents, opponents, and religious and cultural minorities (*FT* 268).

Therefore, the error lies upstream, so to speak, in the fact that the very concept of "legitimate defense" refers to a retributive conception of justice, characterized by the idea of proportionality and reparation for guilt rather than by *forgiveness*.

In this way, the Catholic position on the question of the inviolability of human life acquires greater internal coherence, since it is no longer admissible in any case to intentionally will someone's death, even if the person is an enemy in war or an offender legitimately found guilty. One cannot legitimize violence on the basis of the wrong suffered. One cannot say that

---

assumed, or potential. The third condition is that defensive violence must be proportionate; it cannot be greater or cause more harm than the aggressive violence. The second condition affirms the unlawfulness of preventive violence, while the third condition asserts the inadmissibility of recourse to vindictive violence. Cf. C. Schönborn, *Scegli la vita. La morale cristiana secondo il Catechismo della Chiesa cattolica*, Jaca Book, Milano 2000, 126–128.

responding to evil with evil is permissible because the other one started it.

The new and important contribution of Pope Francis on this topic is the affirmation of the inadmissibility of the death penalty in and of itself, without any reservation, and consequently, the firm commitment to its abolition throughout the world.

8.

THE CHURCH AND RELIGIONS SERVING THE UNIVERSAL CALL TO BE SIBLINGS

(*Fratelli Tutti*, ch. 8)

Fratelli Tutti is overall an appeal to humanity to recover the community dimension of life, and life together in civil society. In this effort to bring together the universal "we" inhabiting our common home, chapter 8 of the encyclical makes *an appeal within an appeal*; that is, Pope Francis invites religions to contribute decisively to defending social justice and building up our universally being siblings (*FT* 271).

What was described at the beginning of *Fratelli Tutti* as a *dream* in the rich biblical sense (*FT* 4) now envisions an interfaith "synodality." This would be walking together as believers, without losing one's respective religious identity, but focusing on a common goal, that of joining forces so that unity prevails over division, love over hatred, and peace over war.

In this final section of the encyclical, all the themes developed in the preceding chapters converge. A new style of Magisterium seems to take shape. As Saint Paul VI pointed out, "Merely to remain true to the faith is not enough" (*ES* 64). In other words, it is not enough to repeat the doctrine that has been codified by Tradition; rather, it is necessary to situate the everlasting truth in contemporary history, to make the present fruitful with a life-giving vision of the future. From Francis's "new vision" or dream (*FT* 6) emerges a utopian tension capable of remodeling[1] the Petrine ministry itself as a service to unity that goes beyond the confines of the Catholic Church and extends to humanity.[2] Transmitting the living substance of the Gospel, therefore, not only requires consolidating the capacity to examine critically today's conditions and possibilities for "handing on tradition" (*paradosis*), but it also means increasing its ability to reach out, that is, to allow the dialoguing attitude of faith and the force of attraction exercised by the proclamation of the Gospel to go beyond concern to have the Church's superiority recognized over other religions.

A paradigmatic change can be found embedded in the ecclesiology developed at Vatican II. Rethinking the Church as an event of communion entails inwardly (*ad intra*) the harmonization of different transcultural models in a more attentive listening to the faithful's sense of the faith (*sensus fidei fidelium*); it entails outwardly (*ad extra*) the willingness to turn to the world, renouncing a judgmental stance, in an openness to an equal encounter that begins with an effective respect for the other's diversity, seen not as a threat from which to protect oneself, but as a gift that reflects the truth projected by the mystery of God.

---

[1] In *Evangelii Gaudium*, Pope Francis outlined the need and urgency to consider "a conversion of the papacy" (*EG* 32).

[2] Saint Paul VI had expressed the conviction that dialogue should characterize and reconfigure the apostolic office of the successors of Peter (*ES* 69). In his encyclical *Ut Unum Sint*, Saint John Paul II, echoing the desire of many Christians belonging both to the Orthodox "sister Churches" and to the Lutheran confessions, also pointed to the grounds for rethinking the exercise of the Petrine ministry with a view to ecumenical unity: "As Bishop of Rome I am fully aware, as I have reaffirmed in the present Encyclical Letter, that Christ ardently desires the full and visible communion of all those Communities in which, by virtue of God's faithfulness, his Spirit dwells. I am convinced that I have a particular responsibility in this regard, above all in acknowledging the ecumenical aspirations of the majority of the Christian Communities and in heeding the request made of me to find a way of exercising the primacy which, while in no way renouncing what is essential to its mission, is nonetheless open to a new situation" (*UuS* 95).

Interreligious dialogue and our all being siblings:
The relevance of the Declaration **Nostra Aetate**

The arguments developed in chapter 8 of *Fratelli Tutti* are a litmus test of the declaration *Nostra Aetate*, with which Vatican II undertook to specify the nature of the relations between the Catholic Church and non-Christian religions.[3]

Nostra Aetate grounds our Christian understanding of the relationship between the Catholic Church and other religions, what all persons and all peoples have in common in a twofold way: our common origin from God, and our common destiny in God, according to the divine plan of salvation for humanity.[4] In other words, Christian self-awareness is called to hold together, in a dynamic tension, these two constitutive elements of its identity. On the one hand, the certitude that in Jesus is given the full and definitive revelation of God, and so he is the "one mediator between God and men" (1 Tim 2:5). On the other hand, the certitude that God wants all humans to be saved (1 Tim 2:4)

---

[3] The final text of the Declaration *Nostra Aetate* was approved on October 28, 1965, during the pontificate of Saint Paul VI. The initial draft elaborated in 1961, called *Decretum de Judaeis*, focused on the relationship between the Catholic Church and the Jewish religion. The main difficulty to overcome was the long-time accusation of deicide that had been leveled against the Jewish people. The decision of the Council Fathers to free the Jewish people from the accusation of having condemned Jesus Christ to the torture of the Cross, and of bearing the guilt of his innocent death, marked a fundamental step in the fight against anti-Semitism and racism, on which Pope Pius XI had also expressed himself. But the declaration soon took on a very different shape compared to the initial draft, expanding its scope to examine the problem of relations between the Catholic Church and non-Christian religions more generally. Even more than to Judaism, the declaration was a positive development with respect to Islam. For, for the first time in the history of the Church's Magisterium, Islam was taken into consideration as an object of attention and, given their common Abrahamic heritage, was described in its relation to Christianity. Cf. R. De Mattei, *Il Concilio Vaticano II. Una storia mai scritta*, Lindau, Torino 2019, 485–490.

[4] Cf. C. Geffré, "La vérité du Christianisme à l'âge du pluralisme religieux," in *Angelicum* 74 (1997): 171–191.

and for this reason makes himself present to them in myriad ways (*LG* 16; *GS* 22), not only to individuals who implicitly and subjectively respond to the promptings of grace, but—as John Paul II would later insist in *Redemptoris Missio*—to entire peoples, cultures, and religious traditions (*RM* 28).[5]

To hold these polarities together without canceling each other out, Vatican II invites us to fix our gaze on the self-emptying (*kenosis*) of Jesus Christ. The mystery of his death and resurrection, in which the unique form of God's action toward humanity is manifested, is the necessary and decisive criterion of judgment and truth that illuminates the soteriological meaning of religions on the path toward salvation.[6]

With *Nostra Aetate*, therefore, the Council Fathers pronounced themselves in favor of a substantially positive evaluation of religions and concluded that they "often reflect a ray of that Truth which enlightens all men" (*NA* 2). Although prudence still led the Fathers to prefer a negative formulation, this statement was a break and marked a turning point in the Church's self-understanding: For the first time, in an explicit and authoritative way, the possibility of salvation outside of its visible boundaries was recognized.[7]

---

[5] Cf. P. Trianni, *Nostra Aetate: alle radici del dialogo interreligioso,* Lateran University Press, Città del Vaticano 2016.

[6] The Declaration of the Congregation for the Doctrine of the Faith *Dominus Iesus*, starting from the conviction that God's universal salvific will is offered and fulfilled once and for all in the Paschal Mystery of Christ, reiterates that "theology today, in its reflection on the existence of other religious experiences and on their meaning in God's salvific plan, is invited to explore if and in what way the historical figures and positive elements of these religions may fall within the divine plan of salvation" (*DI* 14). In his Apostolic Letter *Novo Millennio Ineunte*, Saint John Paul II also called for a renewed theological reflection that is consistent with the teachings of the Council. He affirmed: "In the common experience of humanity, for all its contradictions, the Spirit of God, who 'blows where he wills' (*Jn* 3:8), not infrequently reveals signs of his presence which help Christ's followers to understand more deeply the message which they bear" (*NmI* 56).

[7] *Lumen Gentium* affirms that "the unique mediation of the Redeemer does not exclude but rather gives rise to a manifold cooperation which is but

The Council made its pastoral intent clear when it proposed dialogue as necessary above all for the Church itself. Dialogue allows it to appreciate the values that emerge in other religions, from their tacit orientation to Christ through the mysterious action of the Spirit (*RM* 29). This necessity of dialogue was further expressed in the Council's understanding that guiding peoples to the realization of all being siblings is an integral part of the mission entrusted to the Church by the Risen Lord. If the essential nature of Christian identity resides in our relationship with Christ—who is the *form* of the revelation of the one and triune God—in the very act of welcoming and giving ourselves to others, then interreligious dialogue springs from that same necessity of proclaiming the Gospel.[8]

It is worth dwelling on this last point, because when the Second Vatican Council became aware that nations and peoples were so close to one another that dialogue between the Catholic Church and other religions had become a real necessity, it undertook a careful reflection on the subject, opening a perspective that was historically unprecedented. Far from presenting dialogue in a functional way, as unavoidable albeit expedient, the Council Fathers saw the foundation of dialogue in the communion of love among the three Divine Persons of the Trinity.

---

a sharing in this one source" (*LG* 62). The Church is therefore the necessary means for the salvation of all, even those who do not believe in Christ. However, the perspective inaugurated by *Nostra Aetate* does not limit itself to examining the question of the salvation of non-Christians, but explores on a theoretical and practical level the much broader significance of the various world religions within God's plan for humanity. Cf. J. Dupuis, *Verso una teologia cristiana del pluralismo religioso,* Queriniana, Brescia 1997, 173–180; cf. P. Rossano, "Lo Spirito Santo nelle religioni e nelle culture non cristiane," in idem, *Dialogo e annunciocristiano. L'Incontro con le grandi religioni,* Edizioni Paoline, Cinisello Balsamo, 85–97; cf. F. Gaiffi, "Il pluralismo religioso nella riflessione teologica recente: un'appendice bibliografica," in *Il pluralismo religioso. Una prospettiva interdisciplinare,* ed. A. Fabris and M. Gronchi, San Paolo, Cinisello Balsamo 1998, 203–226.

[8] Cf. P. Coda, "Religioni (teologia delle)," in *Dizionario Critico di Teologia,* ed. P. Coda, Borla/Città Nuova, Roma 2005, 1122–1127.

This theological foundation, underlined by the Council, opened up a renewed vision of our all being siblings (*NA* 5).

Interreligious dialogue and the proclamation of the Gospel are not contradictory, but aspects of the one evangelizing mission of the Church (*RM* 20). Indeed, these two elements must preserve their intimate bond and, at the same time, their distinctiveness, so that they are neither confused, nor considered equivalent, nor made use of for other reasons.

It remains to be clarified *how* to carry out this mission and *in what way* to interpret the task of showing others the way to follow. Should there be some office with a certain authority? Is it enough for religions to relate to the Catholic Church and so imply its excellence? Or is it unnecessary for them to acknowledge it at all?

Fratelli Tutti urges us to rethink the very meaning of the Church's saving mediation. This does not take place by claiming a role of pre-eminence or leadership over other religions.[9] Rather, the Church places itself at their service as "a sign and instrument both of a very closely knit union with God and of the unity of the whole human race" (*LG* 1). Interreligious dialogue presupposes the firm decision to meet our interlocutors with esteem and respect, without any deception or claim of primacy. We recognize one another as *similar*, and we place ourselves on the same level as *siblings* to one another. If, at this historic juncture, we wish to speak of a role of *guidance*, then it

---

[9] In theological discussions on the dialogue between religions, three perspectives have been put forward, both inside and outside the Church. The first is ecclesiocentric or even exclusivist—following the well-known adage "No salvation outside the Church" (*Salus extra ecclesiam non est*)—tending to deny any value to non-Christian religions. This conception is now outdated. The second perspective is christocentric or inclusivist, seeking to highlight the action of Christ in other religions. This vision is still relevant and includes several variants. The third perspective is theocentric or pluralist, aiming to recognize the theological and objective value of each religion based on the conviction that God speaks in diverse ways and places. Cf. E. Echevarria, "The Salvation of Non-Christians? Reflections on Vatican II's *Gaudium et Spes* 22, *Lumen Gentium* 16, Gerald O'Collins, S.J., and St. John Paul II," in *Angelicum* 94, no. 1 (2017): 93–142.

will consist in the willingness to call the other religions to dialogue, initiating processes, creating opportunities for meeting, and supporting that gradual journey of maturation that enables everyone to encounter all others as equals.

Understood in this way, the task of guiding others implies for the Catholic Church a willingness to open up, renouncing any pretensions to an asymmetrical or special status and assuming a humble, sincere, and discreet attitude. This entails a decision to not consider itself above others, and also a determination to engage in dialogue at the cost of starting at a disadvantage — namely, without necessarily demanding reciprocity. Indeed, while reciprocity is desirable, it is not a necessary condition for dialogue in the Christian sense, since Christ died for all (2 Cor 5:15), giving himself even for his enemies (Mt 5:44–45). The dynamic tension toward communion and mutual recognition must not falter when reciprocity is compromised or even denied.

Human dignity and autonomous reason: The need to recover the transcendent foundation of the human being

In *Nostra Aetate*, the Council chose to reflect on religions by focusing its gaze on "the whole human race" (*NA* 1), emphasizing first and foremost its uniqueness compared with the rest of creation and its constant search for meaning and direction. The Council Fathers noted that from time immemorial human beings have sought to respond "to the unsolved riddles of the human condition" (*NA* 1). From ancient times, the uninterrupted presence of a "profound religious sense" testifies to "a certain perception of that hidden power" (*NA* 2) that pervades nature and acts in it.

The Council Fathers also pointed out how this innate inclination to express oneself in religious beliefs has also been developed and refined in relation to the progress of civilizations. As a historical and cultural expression, religion also shows humanity's ongoing effort to respond to existential questions "by means of more refined concepts and a more developed language" (*NA* 2).

The Council thus underlines the radical and inescapable "ontological question" of existence that inhabits the human heart, compelling us to ask questions about the origin and goal of our life, about the first and last principles that account for all that exists. *Nostra Aetate* points to this as the fundamental and foundational horizon of every religion.

With this viewpoint, the Council took up the Augustinian heritage of the restless heart (*inquietum cor*)[10] as an imprint that God's creative hand has impressed upon the human person, as well as the Scholastic tradition that recognized human beings as inhabited by a natural desire to see God (*naturale desiderium videndi Deum*).[11] At the basis of this questioning, every human being perceives, though not always clearly, the presence of Someone who questions one and calls one to account for the generous gift of existence.

As *Gaudium et Spes* affirms: "Conscience is the most secret core and sanctuary of a man. There he is alone with God, Whose voice echoes in his depths" (*GS* 16). In other words, conscience is where the original revelation of God takes place, where every person can come to know that he or she is made to relate to Another and is thus essentially called to responsibility.[12]

The horizon opened up by *Fratelli Tutti* finds its roots in *Nostra Aetate* and highlights the element that is common among all religions: the "filial" recognition that we as human beings are creatures called to transcend ourselves and the physical universe in our relationship with God. On the basis of this primary anthropological conviction, all religions affirm their fundamental "respect for each human person" (*FT* 271).

---

[10] Augustine of Hippo, *Confessions*, XI, 2, 3.

[11] Cf. Thomas Aquinas, *Summa Theologiae*, I, q.12, a.1.

[12] Cf. G. Scattolin, "Spiritualità in dialogo o la spiritualità come terreno comune di dialogo interreligioso," in *Divus Thomas* 110, no. 3 (2007): 190–221.

For Pope Francis, the original contribution of religion to today's culture is precisely the inherent openness to transcendence. Indeed, reminding the people of our time that their being is intrinsically oriented to the Absolute, which calls beyond the sphere of merely material realities, is an irreplaceable service to the world. Recognizing ourselves as creatures before God, and as sons and daughters destined to be fulfilled by love in the relationship to which God invites us, can sustain and hasten the achievement of peace among nations and the pursuit of true equality among human beings.

Reason alone, as we can see on closer examination, has proven capable of affirming equality among human beings, but it has also proven insufficient for justifying the foundation of our all being siblings (*FT* 272).

The Enlightenment solemnly affirmed the primacy of subjectivity. In so doing, it affirmed that reason is autonomous from religion and any other form of institutional authority related to it. In the field of ethics, this means that the individual subject can determine what is normative, since reason alone is considered capable of discerning the good to be pursued and of establishing laws that are suited to regulate human behavior.[13] Even when considering the community as a moral subject, ethical normativity is anchored in the rationality that is common to all human beings, thus establishing universally valid laws. However, since it is subjectivity—whether individual or on the group level—that serves as the foundation for ethics, any authentic relationship with the other is compromised at the outset. This limits the realities to which normativity could potentially be applied, leaving it susceptible to arbitrary and self-referential applications.[14]

---

[13] Cf. V. Possenti, "Alle sorgenti dell'etica. Il problema dell'autonomia morale," in *Rivista di Filosofia Neo-Scolastica* 78, no. 3 (1986): 449–481.

[14] Cf. M. C. Donadío Maggi de Gandolfi, "Crisis de la razón humana y su restauración en la cultura contemporánea," in *Divus Thomas* 121, no. 3 (2018): 156–166.

Religions, by contrast, presuppose the existence of an eternal Truth that is the basis of ethical normativity, without which humanity can neither arrive at the truth about itself, or even guarantee the objectivity of what is good. Quoting *Centesimus Annus*, Pope Francis recalls that when reference to transcendent truth is denied, "there is no sure principle for guaranteeing just relations between people" (*CA* 44; *FT* 273). In this sense, the totalitarian regimes of the twentieth century were an expression of what can happen when humanity abandons itself to "self-sufficient" reason; the dramatic and unprecedentedly violent outcomes witnessed during the last century depended on a disavowal of the transcendent foundation of the dignity of the human person.

This is why Pope Francis is convinced that "our witness to God benefits our societies" (*FT* 274). By their unique contribution, religions offer a description of the human person as "other" that rescues us from the risks represented by reductionism of various kinds. Thus, interreligious dialogue "does not take place simply for the sake of diplomacy, consideration, or tolerance" (*FT* 271), but because sharing spiritual experiences, openly seeking the truth, and cooperating in works of charity can transmit spiritual and moral values, principles, and ideals to civil society that it would otherwise be lacking.

Church, religions, and political community: The public relevance of the "experiential treasure" of religions

We need to question ourselves today as human beings about the meaning of our existence and to get back in touch with that inner dimension which questions us about the meaning of life. This urgent need points to the relevance of interreligious dialogue for our present era. Contemporary culture has marginalized religious questions, deeming them mostly irrelevant, or even attempting to eliminate them from the horizon of human understanding, substituting for them a notion of progress that implies an inevitable emancipation from God.[15]

For this reason, Pope Francis sees that one of the most important causes of the crises of our modern world is "a desensitized human conscience, a distancing from religious values" (*FT* 275).

Religions oppose this nihilistic tendency, offering an alternative to those anthropological theories that disavow the transcendent foundation of the human. By questioning the idea that human beings can only be fulfilled by distancing themselves from anything religious, religions enter into critical dialogue with the dominant culture, which toes the Enlightenment and secularist line.[16]

Pope Francis notes with disappointment that only "the powerful and 'experts'" seem to have a voice in public debate, while no room is given for "reflections born of religious traditions that are the repository of centuries of experience and wisdom" (*FT* 275). It is often forgotten that classical religious texts can offer meaning that is relevant for every era, because they stimulate awareness and thought insofar as they convey "principles which are profoundly humanistic" (*EG* 256).

The predominant rationalism of our time, which is rooted in "prevailing individualism accompanied by materialistic philosophies" (*FT* 275), has discredited religion, judging that what it has to offer to humanity is narrow-minded and deliberately confusing.

There are those who believe that relativism, skepticism, and agnosticism constitute the approach most appropriate for democracy, and that those who believe in an objective truth are to

---

[15] Cf. P. Dominici, "La modernità complessa tra istanze di emancipazione e derive dell'individualismo: la comunicazione per il 'legame sociale,'" in *Studi di sociologia* 52, no. 3 (2014): 281–304.

[16] Cf. H. Joas, *Valori, società, religione*, ed. U. Perone, Rosenberg and Sellier, Torino 2014, 61–86.

be considered unfit for political life, because they do not accept that truth depends on the decisions of the majority.[17]

However, delegitimizing the message of religion is not only a way of evading confrontation and imposing a dictatorship of worldly and material values, but it is also a way of weakening social life because, if there is no ultimate truth, then political action can easily be made use of for the sake of power.[18]

Pope Francis, for his part, claims that the Church has a public role and participates actively in the building of a more just world of siblings (*FT* 276). That it is appropriate for the Church to intervene in areas that are not immediately religious flows from the conviction that no field that concerns the human can be considered extraneous to its interest (*GS* 1).[19] Not even science and politics can be considered autonomous and "absolute" with respect to the ethical and moral evaluation of the choices they intend to make. On these important ethical considerations, the Church and religious traditions in general must be free to express themselves without being accused of meddling in areas that do not concern them.[20]

---

[17] It would be harmful to assume that there is some sort of alliance between democracy and ethical relativism (cf. *Veritatis Splendor* 101), just as it would be harmful to think that "the legal system of any society should limit itself to taking account of and accepting the convictions of the majority" and that legal systems "should therefore be based solely upon what the majority itself considers moral and actually practices" (*Evangelium Vitae* 69). Cf. F. Cannone, "La democrazia nel pensiero di Giovanni Paolo II," in *Angelicum* 85, no. 2 (2008): 557–600.

[18] Cf. A. Lobato, "Gli ostacoli all'incontro con Dio nella cultura odierna," in *Angelicum* 70, no. 2 (1993): 169–206.

[19] Cf. R. Pezzimenti, "La Dottrina Sociale della Chiesa nel quadro del pensiero sociale e politico moderno," in *Angelicum* 70, no. 2 (1993): 169–206.

[20] In *Centesimus Annus*, Saint John Paul II spoke out against a reductive interpretation of the involvement of the Church's Magisterium, affirming instead that "the Church, in fact, has something to say about specific human situations, both individual and communal, national and international. She formulates a genuine doctrine for these situations, a *corpus* which enables her to analyze social realities, to make judgments about them and to indicate directions to be taken for the just resolution of the problems involved" (*CA* 5). In the same

Pope Francis addresses the question of the relationship between Church and politics in order to reaffirm their mutual independence and autonomy, and acknowledges that this distinction does not imply a separation, since both—though in different capacities—are at the service of the personal and social vocation of the one human community (*GS* 76).[21]

However, Francis points out that the recognition, in Church teaching, of the principle of the secularity of the State[22] does not imply that the Church needs to "restrict her mission to the private sphere" (*FT* 276).[23] *Gaudium et Spes* affirmed that a

---

vein, Benedict XVI reiterated that the Church's social teaching is a valid means of contributing "to the purification of reason" (*DCE* 29): indeed, when it comes to providing a concrete response to the demands of justice, practical reason always runs the risk of "a certain ethical blindness caused by the dazzling effect of power and special interests" (*DCE* 28). This is where "politics and faith meet" (*DCE* 28): faith, insofar as it is a true encounter with the living God, can liberate reason from its own blindness and help those involved in politics to remain lucid about all that might conceal the pursuit of partisan interests or the quest for power in any program aimed at achieving justice.

[21] Cf. Pontifical Council, "Justice and Peace," *Compendium of the Social Doctrine of the Church*, nos., 424, 230.

[22] Vatican II expressed an essentially positive evaluation of politics, recognizing both its necessity and its foundation in human nature. The Council affirmed, for example, that among the social bonds that are necessary for the perfecting of the human person, some correspond directly to our innermost nature, and this includes the political community (*GS* 25). For this reason, the Council hoped that peaceful and constructive cooperation would be established between the Church and the political community, so that this may be as beneficial as possible for the good of all citizens, in ways suited to the varied circumstances of place and time (*GS* 76). In this way, the Council Fathers "updated" the official position of the Church in its way of perceiving its relationship with the State, rejecting both the modern ideas of total separation, aggressive anticlericalism, and discriminatory secularism, as well as those that advocated for the State to take on a religious or confessional nature. Cf. R. Rybka, "La laicità dello Stato nella *Gaudium et Spes* e nel *Compendio della Dottrina Sociale della Chiesa*," in *Studi/Contributions* 2 (2015): 42–49.

[23] In particular, those who are critical of the Church see in the exercise of ecclesiastical jurisdiction a way of reaffirming a sort of indirect power in temporal matters (*potestas indirecta in temporalibus*) that would not only remove the Church from the purview of the State, carving out spaces for institutional

defense of the fundamental rights of the human person from a moral perspective, albeit not directly in the political arena, is part of the Church's mission (*GS* 76).

The Church's non-interference in political affairs does not mean failing to express its own point of view or of its concern for integral human development. In fact, according to Church teaching, the political community is fully autonomous and independent in its organization and management, but not completely so when it comes to moral values.[24]

It is not enough for a system to be "democratic" in order for it to pursue the common good. Rather, it is necessary that the dignity and inalienable rights of the human person be effectively respected.[25] The goodness of a democratic system

---

freedom, but which would also allow the Church to exert undue interference in the affairs of the State. According to this way of thinking, it would be fitting that the Church's freedom and power (*libertas-potestas*) be exclusively relegated to the intra-ecclesial sphere, to the "private" internal affairs of the Church. Cf. S. Briccola, "Il potere della Chiesa in ambito temporale esiste ancora?" in *Il Politico* 70, no. 1 (2005): 57–77; cf. V. Ferrone, "La libertà religiosa come fondamento storico della laicità," in *Contemporanea* 10, no. 4 (2007): 670–677.

[24] The *Doctrinal Note on Some Questions Regarding the Participation of Catholics in Political Life*, promulgated in 2002 by the Congregation for the Doctrine of the Faith, stated: "Promoting the common good of society, according to one's conscience, has nothing to do with 'confessionalism' or religious intolerance. For Catholic moral doctrine, the rightful autonomy of the political or civil sphere from that of religion and the Church—*but not from that of morality*—is a value that has been attained and recognized by the Catholic Church and belongs to inheritance of contemporary civilization." Cf. Congregation for the Doctrine of the Faith, *Doctrinal Note on Some Questions Regarding the Participation of Catholics in Political Life*, November 24, 2002, 6.

[25] *Gaudium et Spes* defines the "common good" as "the sum of those conditions of social life which allow social groups and their individual members relatively thorough and ready access to their own fulfillment" (*GS* 26). This initial "formal" definition is then elaborated on in more concrete terms: "Therefore, there must be made available to all men everything necessary for leading a life truly human, such as food, clothing, and shelter; the right to choose a state of life freely and to found a family, the right to education, to employment, to a good reputation, to respect, to appropriate information,

does not depend on respect for mere legalities and for the rules that ensure its organization and functioning, but rather on the recognition of those norms and values that are more important than any particular system of government, values that must be reflected in the direction that politics takes regarding the economy and social coexistence.[26]

For these reasons, the Church, while not engaging in "party politics," cannot "renounce the political dimension of life itself" (*FT* 276) or exempt itself from taking part in it. At the same time, the Church accepts that its public role be limited to intervening in the social fabric exclusively in activities of a charitable or educational nature, taking on the task of "substitution" when the State is lacking in these areas.[27]

---

to activity in accord with the upright norm of one's own conscience, to protection of privacy and rightful freedom even in matters religious" (*GS* 26). Cf. C. Mellon, "Politica (I): la riflessione del Concilio Vaticano II," in *Aggiornamenti Sociali* 12 (2012): 881–884.

[26] Saint John Paul II adds: "Authentic democracy is possible only in a State ruled by law, and on the basis of a correct conception of the human person. It requires that the necessary conditions be present for the advancement both of the individual through education and formation in true ideals, and of the 'subjectivity' of society through the creation of structures of participation and shared responsibility" (*CA* 46).

[27] *Lumen Gentium* assigns lay people the task of dedicating themselves directly and ordinarily to politics, since "what specifically characterizes the laity is their secular nature" (*LG* 31). For ordained ministers, on the other hand, *Lumen Gentium* indicates the ecclesial community as the sphere in which to carry out the pastoral ministry that constitutes their ecclesial specificity (*LG* 20). Furthermore, the Council invites men and women religious to give witness to their specific vocation by anticipating here and now the future condition of the Kingdom of God, in which temporal power will have no place and will become superfluous (*LG* 44; *PC* 1). Indeed, the *Code of Canon Law* clearly states that clerics "are forbidden to assume public offices which entail a participation in the exercise of civil power" (can. 285 §3) and stipulates that they "are not to have an active part in political parties and in governing labor unions unless, in the judgment of competent ecclesiastical authority, the protection of the rights of the Church or the promotion of the common good requires it" (can. 287 §2). Thus, the Church's ministers are discouraged from engaging in "party politics," though that possibility is not categorically excluded. As Pope Francis points out, this does not mean that

Saint John Paul II, in *Sollicitudo Rei Socialis*, affirmed that the Church "does not propose economic and political systems or programs, nor does she show preference for one or the other, provided that human dignity is properly respected and promoted, and provided she herself is allowed the room she needs to exercise her ministry in the world" (*SrS* 41).

The perspective of faith helps to keep alive an awareness of the limitations of politics and protects against the temptation to believe that politics is capable of, as Pope Benedict's Encyclical *Deus Caritas Est* states, "doing what God's governance of the world apparently cannot: fully resolving every problem" (*DCE* 36).

The Gospel is the "source" of Christian identity: Church action to defend religious freedom and promote ecumenical dialogue

The Church should not be afraid to recognize the mysterious action of God in other religions or shy away from appreciating everything that is "true and holy" (*NA* 2) in them. When we are fully aware of our own identity, it is possible to engage in dialogue without falling into some form of relativism[28] or "facile syncretism" (*EG* 251). Creating opportunities for encounters

---

they must distance themselves from political realities and not get involved in the ways and means that concern their pastoral mission.

[28] Benedict XVI likewise affirmed: "For the Church, dialogue between the followers of the different religions represents an important means of cooperating with all religious communities for the common good. . . . *The path to take is not the way of relativism or religious syncretism*. The Church, in fact, proclaims, and is in duty bound to proclaim without fail, Christ who is the way, the truth, and the life (Jn 14:6); in Christ, in whom God reconciled all things to himself, people find the fullness of the religious life. Yet this in no way excludes dialogue and the common pursuit of truth in different areas of life, since, as Saint Thomas Aquinas would say, 'every truth, whoever utters it, comes from the Holy Spirit.'" Cf. Benedict XVI, "Religious Freedom, the Path to Peace," *Message for the XLIV World Day of Peace,* January 1, 2011, 11.

among religions and beginning to collaborate in ways that promote the common good do not mean abdicating one's own convictions or watering down our own credo, because "the deeper, stronger, and richer our own identity is, the more we will be capable of enriching others with our own proper contribution" (*FT* 282).

For these reasons, Christians go forth "to the encounter with the sacred mystery of the other" (*FT* 277), knowing that from the Gospel of Jesus Christ flows our certainty of the dignity of the human person and our awareness of the universal call to be siblings. Indeed, the Church is "catholic" because in every time and place it recognizes itself as the "recipient" of the personal love of God in Christ. At the same time, the Church is "sent" by the power of the Risen Lord to give rise to "a new world, where all of us are brothers and sisters, where there is room for all those whom our societies discard, where justice and peace are resplendent" (*FT* 278).[29]

By remaining firmly rooted in her own identity, the Church can face two further challenges that being siblings and seeking peace present: defending religious freedom and promoting ecumenism.

Religious freedom is a fundamental right that is grounded in the dignity of the human person, whose transcendent nature precedes and transcends any recognition by a society's legal system or positive law.[30]

---

[29] It is interesting to note how in *Fratelli Tutti* 278 the reference to the Virgin Mary is brought back into the context of the discourse on "Catholic" identity, almost as if to underline how devotion to the Mother of God has always been among its characteristic elements. Pope Francis sees in the gift of the Virgin Mary an eloquent sign of God's will to call all of humanity together, so that all men and women may live in communion with God and with one another. Indeed, by dying on the Cross, Christ not only revealed to us the face of the Father, but he also entrusted us to the care of a Mother. As disciples of Jesus, we discover that we are siblings by virtue of God's paternity, but we are also invited to walk the path of siblings all with the support of Mary's motherhood.

[30] Cf. F. Viola, "I diritti umani alla prova del diritto naturale," in *Persona y Derecho* 23, no. 2 (1990): 101–120.

Today's world is characterized by cultural pluralism and, at the same time, finds it hard to recognize human rights everywhere. Yet these are politically fundamental and socially relevant. To affirm these rights, the absence of oppressive and repressive policies is not enough. The right to manifest one's faith, both individually and communally, in public and in private, must also be recognized, without incurring the stigma of social exclusion.[31]

Therefore, religious freedom represents an acquisition of political and juridical civilization, because moving beyond the personal sphere, it is realized in relationship with others. Pope Francis affirms that a peaceful and fruitful coexistence between cultures and religions depends on religious freedom being guaranteed in every nation. Since the path to achieving religious freedom is often arduous, he calls for a minimal principle of reciprocity as an initial step toward respecting religious freedom: "We Christians ask that, in those countries where we are a minority, we be guaranteed freedom, even as we ourselves promote that freedom for non-Christians in places where they are a minority" (*FT* 279).

As an essential good, religious freedom is not the exclusive heritage of believers, but of the entire family of the peoples of the earth: "God's love is the same for everyone, regardless of religion. Even if they are atheists, his love is the same" (*FT* 281). Here Pope Francis echoes the Council's innovative teaching on religious freedom expressed in *Dignitatis Humanae*. In

---

[31] Benedict XVI highlighted the public dimension of religion and the great value that it can offer in overcoming conflicts and restoring peace and justice among peoples, nations, societies, and cultures. Religious freedom "expresses what is unique about the human person, for it allows us to direct our personal and social life to God, in whose light the identity, meaning and purpose of the person are fully understood. To deny or arbitrarily restrict this freedom is to foster a reductive vision of the human person; to eclipse the public role of religion is to create a society which is unjust, inasmuch as it fails to take account of the true nature of the human person; *it is to stifle the growth of the authentic and lasting peace of the whole human family*." Cf. Benedict XVI, "Religious Freedom, The Path to Peace," *Message for the XLIV World Day of Peace,* January 1, 2011, 1.

particular, the Council affirms the principle of the inviolability of the rights of the person (*DH* 1; 6), beginning with freedom of conscience, which must be respected even when the person is considered to have fallen into error.[32]

This ability to regard others benevolently, regardless of who they are and what they believe, is the basic criterion of credibility and coherence to which every religion is subject. That is why no form of contempt and xenophobic hatred, no abominable expression of violence, "has [any] basis in our fundamental religious convictions" (*FT* 282).

The phenomenon of terrorism with a religious origin is also a threat to religious freedom, because it disavows the "moral principle of personal and social responsibility" and does not

---

[32] The traditional position of Catholic theology, strongly conditioned by Canon Law, affirmed that truth was the only acceptable basis for freedom. Therefore, since error was not admissible, it was necessary firmly to condemn those who profess to be atheists or non-believers. In other words, if freedom of conscience leads one to deny the existence of God, then one is obliged to not follow it. In *Pacem in Terris*, however, Saint John XXIII laid the groundwork for a change in this perspective, positing the relevant distinction between error and the person who errs, arguing: "A man who has fallen into error does not cease to be a man. He never forfeits his personal dignity; and that is something that must always be taken into account. Besides, there exists in man's very nature an undying capacity to break through the barriers of error and seek the road to truth" (*PiT* 158). This set the groundwork for the Council's realistic vision, which presupposes the right of the human person to seek the truth, but does not provide a guarantee of obtaining the truth as such. Looking to the work of the Apostles, *Dignitatis Humanae* affirms that they "they showed respect for those who are weak, even though they were in error, and thus they made it plain that 'each one of us is to render to God an account of himself' (Rom 14:12), and for that reason is bound to obey his conscience" (*DH* 11). From this primacy of conscience comes the call for every disciple of Jesus to "love and have prudence and patience in his dealings with those who are in error or in ignorance with regard to the faith" (*DH* 14). The Council does not dismiss the power of truth, nor does it undermine the importance of the Church. Rather, the teachings of the Council place an emphasis on the conditions of history; freedom requires formation, meaning a conscience that is consciously informed by interior discipline. Cf. V. V. Alberti, "La *Dignitatis humanae* e la nuova laicità oltre la rivoluzione e la controrivoluzione," in *Anuario de Historia de la Iglesia* 21 (2012): 303–320.

respect the limits set by the duty to deal with one another "in justice and civility" (*DH* 7). At the origin of every manifestation of terrorism there lies a falsification of God and of life's sacred meaning. When this happens, the truth about the human that is proclaimed by religion becomes enslaved to ideology and is often manipulated by the corrupt interests of politics (*FT* 283; 285).

The pope strongly urges religious leaders not only to distance themselves from and decisively condemn every act of violence and terror committed by these extremist groups, but also to intervene activelty by taking the path of dialogue and "to cooperate in building peace not as intermediaries but as authentic mediators" (*FT* 284).[33]

---

[33] In Catholic theology, the category of *mediation* is used to explain the uniqueness of the saving event that was accomplished in Christ Jesus. He is the center and the foundation of the entire economy of salvation. The uniqueness of this salvific mediation corresponds to the universality of its scope: it is for all people. The mediation of the Church is analogous to, but not univocal with, the mediation of Christ: the Church's mediation derives from the mediation of Christ, but can never be confused with it. Regarding other religions, Saint John Paul II stated: "For [those who do not have the possibility of knowing the Gospel] salvation in Christ is accessible by virtue of a grace which, while having a mysterious relationship to the Church, does not make them formally part of the Church but enlightens them in a way which is accommodated to their spiritual and material situation" (*RM* 10). *Evangelii Gaudium* expands upon this conviction, affirming that, "due to the sacramental dimension of sanctifying grace, God's working in [non-Christian religions] tends to produce signs and rites, sacred expressions which in turn bring others to a communitarian experience of journeying toward God" (*EG* 254). These clarifications are important in contextualizing the distinction between "intermediary" and "mediator" that Pope Francis outlines: "Intermediaries seek to give everyone a discount, ultimately in order to gain something for themselves. The mediator, on the other hand, is one who retains nothing for himself, but rather spends himself generously until he is consumed, knowing that the only gain is peace" (*FT* 284). Pope Francis indicates that the grace of Christ is manifested in religions when they recognize that God calls them to the responsibility of working for peace for our fellow human beings. Implicitly and indirectly, these "practical mediations" aimed at loving one's neighbor associate religion with the unique and universal mediation of Christ.

With regard to ecumenism, on the other hand, *Fratelli Tutti* takes up the perspective opened by Vatican II and deepened by the successive Magisterium,[34] first of all by highlighting the need and urgency of seeking unity among Christians in order to give new vigor to the proclamation of the Gospel.

Unitatis Redintegratio stated that division among Christians not only "openly contradicts the will of Christ," it also "scandalizes the world" (*UR* 1). Pope Francis echoes this decree of Vatican II and notes that "the prophetic and spiritual contribution of unity among Christians" (*FT* 280) is made even more evident by the fragmentation that has resulted from globalization. It is necessary for the various Christian denominations to let their common witness to the love of God overflow in their desire to serve humanity together. Unity among Churches not only makes the Christian proclamation more credible; it is also a significant "contribution to the unity of the human family" (*EG* 245).

For the Council, the renewal of the Church is closely linked with progress in ecumenism (*UR* 6). Likewise, in the area of social teaching and social action, "cooperation among Christians vividly expresses the relationship which in fact already unites them, and it sets in clearer relief the features of Christ the Servant" (*UR* 12). At the same time, the Council Fathers warned that this continual reform to which Christ calls his pilgrim Church cannot take place "without a change of heart" (*UR* 7).

---

[34] Particularly noteworthy is Saint John Paul II's commitment to increasing the ecumenical awareness of the Catholic Church. This is demonstrated by several major events: the promulgation of the *Code of Canons of the Eastern Churches* (October 18, 1990); the intensification of papal trips for ecumenical purposes; the decisive contacts with the Orthodox Churches; the publication of the Apostolic Letter *Lumen Orientale Lumen* (1995) and the Encyclical *Ut Unum Sint* (1995); the *Joint Declaration on the Doctrine of Justification* (October 31, 1999); the drafting and acceptance of the *Ecumenical Charter for the Churches in Europe* (April 22, 2001); and the continuation of the slow work of the theological commissions engaged in bilateral dialogue. Cf. H. Vall Vilardell, "La Spiritualità Ecumenica," in *Gregorianum* 88, no. 2 (2007): 407–420.

This is the reason that led the Council to identify a significant spiritual life as the foundation of ecumenical practice: "This change of heart and holiness of life, along with public and private prayer for the unity of Christians, should be regarded as the soul of the whole ecumenical movement" (*UR* 8).[35] This demands both mutual understanding among the Churches (*UR* 9) and appropriate efforts to express the mysteries of the faith "more profoundly and precisely" (*UR* 11).

In this sense, authentic ecumenical spirituality must draw fully from the richness of the whole ecclesial tradition and value the depth of the different rites and theologies developed within each local Church. Thus, the conciliar Decree *Orientalium Ecclesiarum* affirms that the Catholic Church recognizes the spiritual and ecclesial patrimony of the Eastern Churches as "the heritage of the universal Church" (*OE* 5), adopting the principle that the universal includes the particular without absorbing it. For Pope Francis, this unity in diversity is the path of communion that the Lord continually asks us to set out on: "If we really believe in the abundantly free working of the Holy Spirit, we can learn so much from one another! It is not just about being better informed about others, but rather about reaping what the Spirit has sown in them, which is also meant to be a gift for us" (*EG* 246).

Unity in prayer is a practical ideal, a way of overcoming the objections and reservations that continue to persist on a doctrinal level: "The theological and ecclesiological issues

---

[35] The Council recognized that "human powers and capacities cannot achieve this holy objective" of reconciling all Christians in the unity of the one and only Church of Christ (*UR* 24). Thus, the Council Fathers wished to emphasize at the end of the decree the need for divine intervention for Christian unity to be achieved, placing all their hope in "the prayer of Christ for the Church" (*UR* 24). The same attitude of confident trust is found in several of Pope Francis's addresses. For example, in his meeting with Bartholomew I, patriarch of Constantinople, the pope hinted at the difficulties of walking together as Christians, while at the same time declaring that the hope of succeeding "is founded, not upon us or our poor efforts, but rather upon God's faithfulness." Cf. Francis, *Address of the Holy Father at the Ecumenical Prayer during the Apostolic Journey to Turkey,* November 29, 2014.

that still keep us apart can only be resolved in the course of the journey along this common path."[36] Pope Francis affirms that the differences that separate us will never, in fact, be resolved if we stand still, but only if each one encounters the other, committing to setting aside the misunderstandings, hostilities, and prejudices that have for centuries plagued relations between the Churches. Therefore, they are not to wait for the resolution of theological problems in order to work together, but rather proclaim, pray, and collaborate side by side, in the certainty that "unity is achieved by walking forward."[37]

In a world torn apart by wars, hatred, nationalism, and divisions, Christian communities are called to defend the demands of justice in a spirit of solidarity that takes the side of those who suffer. However, it is not possible to work for justice alone; we must seek it *together*, putting aside all fears and sparing no effort. This is why Pope Francis encourages us not to be afraid to spend ourselves for the sake of a better world: "Let us not be afraid to operate at a loss! Ecumenism is 'a great enterprise operating at a loss.' But the loss is evangelical, reflecting the words of Jesus: 'Those who want to save their life will lose it, and those who lose their life for my sake will save it' (Lk 9:24). To save only what is ours is to walk according to the flesh; to lose everything in the footsteps of Jesus is to walk in the Spirit."[38]

The pope reminds those who would slow down the path of visible unity that there is an ecumenism already "achieved": "Let us see what we can do concretely, rather than grow discouraged about what we cannot. Let us also look to our many brothers and sisters in various parts of the world, particularly in the Middle East, who suffer because they are Christians.

---

[36] Francis, *Address of the Holy Father to Members of the Ecumenical Delegation from Finland,* January 19, 2019.

[37] Francis, *Words of the Holy Father after the Signing of the Joint Declaration with Patriarch Kirill,* La Havana, February 12, 2016.

[38] Francis, *Homily of the Holy Father at the Ecumenical Prayer during the Ecumenical Pilgrimage to Geneva to Mark the 70th Anniversary of the Foundation of the World Council of Churches,* June 21, 2018.

Let us draw close to them. May we never forget that our ecumenical journey is preceded and accompanied by an ecumenism already realized, the ecumenism of blood, which urges us to go forward."[39]

---

[39] Francis, *Address of the Holy Father at the Ecumenical Meeting during the Ecumenical Pilgrimage to Geneva to Mark the 70th Anniversary of the Foundation of the World Council of Churches,* June 21, 2018.

CONCLUSION

In the Magisterium of Pope Francis, his teaching, gradually unfolding over time in words and deeds, finds a moment of synthesis in *Fratelli Tutti*. With various authoritative expressions along the way, his teaching's internal coherence is easily grasped by reading the encyclical in the light of the first words that Jorge Mario Bergoglio pronounced on the evening of his election to the papacy. Before the joyous crowd that filled Saint Peter's Square, he bowed his head and asked everyone to pray that God would grant the whole world the gift of "a great spirit of fraternity."[1] After pointing to faith as the light that illuminates the whole of human existence (*Lumen Fidei*), and to the Gospel as the joy that enlivens our life (*Evangelii Gaudium*), and after pointing to integral ecology as an urgent priority for our time (*Laudato Si'*) and as a challenge for the inculturation of the faith (*Querida Amazonia*), the pope invites us to appreciate more deeply what it means to recognize "our common home" and the consequences, not only on the intra-ecclesial and ecumenical level, but likewise for social coexistence and peace among peoples (*FT* 1).

For the Church today, seeing "siblings all" as a dynamic and open reality offers an authentic path for proclaiming and transmitting the Gospel. Handing on the message of the Crucified and Risen Christ to new generations, to the people of our time, is no longer thinkable merely as an act of "informing" others, that is, simply an act of communicating the truths of our

---

[1] Francis, *First Greeting of the Holy Father Pope Francis*, March 13, 2013, Libreria Editrice Vaticana.

faith about the mystery of the living God. Rather, it involves how the believer takes a stand in relation to the otherness of the world and of one's fellow human beings. This means "putting on Christ" (Rom 13:14) in order to live out a genuinely evangelical style (*EG* 67; 168).

Fratelli Tutti boldly brings together two terms that may seem opposed to one another: *friendship* and *society*. When we speak of friendship, we usually mean a "selective" form of love: we choose our friends, we select them to be our peers. Oftentimes we distinguish the sphere of friendly relationships, which we see as "private," from the social context in which we find ourselves involved with people who seem "imposed" on us from the outside. The message of the encyclical aims to offer humanity a "new vision" or dream (*FT* 6): to act toward others, both near and far, as if we were choosing them as our siblings and friends. This is why Pope Francis opted not to specify the encyclical's addressees, not to limit them to the baptized faithful, but to expand the scope of its message to all people.[2] Pope Francis wants to provide a social teaching that speaks not only to Catholics, but that is capable of guiding everyone, of bringing about "the rebirth of a universal aspiration to fraternity" (*FT* 8).

The Holy Father invites believers—Catholics and those of any other religion—to broaden the very concept of "fraternity," in order to recognize as "siblings" not only those who share the same religious background, but all people, without any exception. The pope asks non-believers and those who do not subscribe to any "credo" to bring a spirit of all siblings to the

---

[2] This choice to address all people should be read in continuity with the turning point brought about by Vatican II. In fact, *Gaudium et Spes* states that the Gospel message "holds true not only for Christians, but for all men of good will in whose hearts grace works in an unseen way. For, since Christ died for all men, and since the ultimate vocation of man is in fact one, and divine, we ought to believe that the Holy Spirit in a manner known only to God offers to every man the possibility of being associated with this paschal mystery" (*GS* 22).

very heart of social life, living out in a secular way the values and ethical principles that are as treasures of religion.

The teaching of Pope Francis, while animated by a precise inner logic, is also in continuity with the unbroken and official doctrine of the Church, especially in its revival of the *inductive* method proposed by the Second Vatican Council.

Gaudium et Spes articulates the exercise of evangelical discernment, the faithful's sense of the faith, the *sensus fidei fidelium*, in three stages: *scrutinizing* the signs of the times; *interpreting* them in the light of the Gospel; and *responding* to questions of meaning (*GS* 4). The text of this pastoral constitution of Vatican II states that faith is nourished by reading history and notes that "since the Church has a visible and social structure as a sign of her unity in Christ, she can and ought to be enriched by the development of human social life" (*GS* 44).

Fratelli Tutti takes this same approach, first in choosing to "hear, distinguish, and interpret the many voices of our age," and also in the call to human social life as the "place" in which the Church can know itself more deeply in the "constitution given her by Christ." In this way "she can understand it more penetratingly, express it better, and adapt it more successfully to our times" (*GS* 44).

Pope Francis points to being siblings and social friendship as a form of love that urges us to get beyond our shortsighted partisan interests in order to include others in our understanding of "good" and of "well-being." Charity, in its capacity to "embrace everything" (*FT* 164), thus becomes the key to sustaining integral human development.

Charity is inclusive and life-giving (*FT* 165) but also open to everyone and common to all (*FT* 183–184). In its light, *Fratelli Tutti* touches upon and weaves together every major theme of the social teaching of the Church: the dignity of the human person and the right to integral development (*FT* 106); the principles of solidarity (*FT* 114–115) and subsidiarity (*FT* 175; 187); the universal destination of goods and private property (*FT* 118–121; 143); work and freedom of enterprise (*FT* 122;

162); international cooperation (*FT* 132); secularity and the relationship between the Church and the political community (*FT* 276); and the right to religious freedom (*FT* 276).

To this are added the condemnation of every kind of war and every misleading ideology that aims to sustain "the possibility of a 'just war'" (*FT* 258). It likewise rejects the death penalty (*FT* 269) and human trafficking (*FT* 24).

The encyclical also identifies concrete steps to be taken, commitments to be made, and concerted efforts to undertake in social, political, and economic spheres: migration (*FT* 38; 128–132); good governance in politics (*FT* 180–182); hunger in the world (*FT* 189); dialogue and social peace (*FT* 217); nuclear disarmament and the collective will for self-restraint in military affairs (*FT* 262); the need for a global agreement to invest resources in health worldwide and in world security (*FT* 173–174); the ecumenical path toward Christian unity (*FT* 280); and the commitment of religions to contribute to the common good and to place themselves at the service of our all being siblings (*FT* 271; 281–285).

Since "great changes are not produced behind desks or in offices" (*FT* 231) but are brought about by concrete gestures and actions, the encyclical takes a practical approach to today's problems and suggests concrete approaches to enhance social coexistence: preserving the memory of the past; being open to dialogue in the present; planning together for the future; initiating processes of reconciliation; and treasuring and safeguarding diversity.

For the Church's witness not to be neglected as insignificant, we need to "scrutinize" the present and undertake an objective and realistic analysis of the evils pervading our time. *Laudato Si'* already spoke out, identifying the causes of the current ecological crisis in a certain use of technology (*LS* 106) and denouncing the irresponsible choices of politics that lets itself be enslaved by the interests of finance (*LS* 109). *Fratelli Tutti* confirms the substantial difference in Francis's teaching compared with the approach taken by the previous Magisterium: it is no longer a question of making the economy more moral, of rendering capitalism more compassionate or comprehending, but rather of "redefining our notion of progress" (*LS* 194), totally transforming the look and order of the world.

To avoid "dealing merely with symptoms" (*LS* 9), it is necessary to rethink the economic model from the bottom up, starting with the centrality of the person and human dignity as the "frontier" of the future (*FT* 22). For these reasons, Pope Francis invites Western countries to recover those instruments they already possess, through history and tradition, in order to reaffirm the inalienable value of the human person (*FT* 40).

On the ideological level, the economy of mere profit is grounded in various reductive anthropologies. This leads to a loss of equity or fairness—not only on a material level, blocking access to basic necessities, but further undermining efforts to ensure respect for the fundamental rights of all human beings throughout the world.

The poor, by their very presence, call into question the cultural status or universe of the West. It is precisely for this reason that there is a tendency to exclude them, to remove them from "our" history and the "reassuring" narrative that we construct for future generations. From the very beginning, the Magisterium of Pope Francis has denounced the culture of indifference[3] and the throwaway culture,[4] pinpointing the many forms of marginalization that infest our time: economic, social, political, existential, and spiritual peripheries.

If salvation history can be understood in terms of God's continuing dialogue with humanity (*DV* 2), then the role and mission of the Catholic Church is to be an expression and actualization of that dialogue. Saint Paul VI affirmed that "the Church must enter into dialogue with the world in which it lives" (*ES* 65), renewing its presence and its action in order

---

[3] Francis, *Homily at the "Arena" Sports Camp in the Salina Quarter during His Visit to Lampedusa*, July 8, 2013, Libreria Editrice Vaticana.

[4] Francis, *Address during the Visit to the Community of Varginha (Manguinhos) on the Apostolic Journey to Rio de Janeiro on the Occasion of the XXVIII World Youth Day*, July 25, 2013, Libreria Editrice Vaticana; cf. *LS* 16; 22; 43.

to overcome effectively every kind of historico-cultural or socio-theological prejudice. In *Fratelli Tutti*, Pope Francis adds that such an attitude of dialogue on the part of the Church can encourage other religions to overcome intolerance, racism, and fundamentalism. This change in perspective leads the Church to embrace the promotion of peace, the struggle for justice, and the defense of human rights as constitutive aspects of the mission of proclaiming the Gospel.

Animated by Christ's love, which is for everyone, the Church becomes a universal sacrament of communion, a gift of salvation that extends beyond its own visible boundaries. If charity unfolds as the capacity to welcome others more and more, then the evangelizing mission of the Church as the People of God on its way is at the service of universal concord and peace among peoples, cultures, and religions.

Instead of expressing an "ideology" of dialogue and of sharing, *Fratelli Tutti* chooses to let real phenomena be its measure. The encyclical avoids the temptation of taking an idealistic approach to peace and instead emphasizes the importance of conflict as a typical dynamic to be expected whenever differences encounter one another. At the same time, Francis asks that confrontation not give way to mutual indifference or to antagonism—which in turn can lead to war—but rather let it give rise to life-giving processes. If dialogue takes conflict on and resolves it positively, then it creates the conditions for experiences of cooperation to take place. Seeking the way of sharing requires everyone to exercise self-restraint, that is, setting oneself limits in order to make space for the other. To disclose one's own limitations as a condition for interaction is to make ourselves vulnerable. For no genuine encounter is possible unless there is willingness to be encountered and understood by the other, and unless we have really decided to let others express themselves. Vulnerability, then, also means choosing to withdraw to some extent, to maintain a bit of autonomy in order not to overwhelm others and respectfully welcome their identity.

In this way, to dialogue is to cultivate the art of approaching or drawing near. We get as close as possible without losing ourselves. We share something because we value the "limiting" difference of the other positively. This is not an easy path at a time when we often tend to use exclusion in order to emphasize the perception of "we." We continue to generate differences, to fuel narratives that demonize on the basis of race, leading to paranoid policies that are obsessed with protecting and immunizing ourselves from foreign "invaders."

If, on the one hand, the vision of *Fratelli Tutti* is attentive to socio-political and cultural dimensions, on the other hand, the arguments establishing the core idea of siblings all are rooted in a solid theological foundation. This theological foundation is fully revealed only at the end of the encyclical, though its implications are present throughout the text: the condition of human beings as siblings flows from the revelation of the true face of God the Father in Christ through the Holy Spirit. The relationships of *agape* within the Holy Trinity teach us that unity does not mean eliminating differences but reciprocal sharing of identities.

But it is also the ecclesiology of *communion*, based on the work of the Incarnate Word, that forms the theological perspective underlying *Fratelli Tutti*. The Church realizes itself by placing itself at the service of humanity and mediates salvation in Christ in its constant commitment to making the Kingdom of God present among people, calling them to be siblings all.

The voice of Pope Francis comes from "the ends of the earth"[5] even if speaking "from the center." It is the voice of a Church that hears the cry of the last, the excluded, the "voiceless." At the same time, let us recognize that one of the many paradoxes of being pope in our time is that the Holy Father is often obliged to speak to the world through the microphone of his adversaries. To ignore the urgent appeal of the desperate is to live as a Church without Christ. So too, to misconstrue

---

[5] Francis, *First Greeting of the Holy Father Pope Francis*.

Francis's teaching by setting it in opposition to the Tradition is to disregard the preferential option that Vatican II made in favor of the poor.

Thus, it is necessary to shun the temptation of indifference that leads one to think and say, "This encyclical is not for us!" It is pertinent in this sense to recall the Council's reaffirmation that bishops are called to teach in communion with the Roman Pontiff "even when he is not speaking *ex cathedra*," and to strive to ensure that the lay faithful develop a mature religious assent "of mind and will" to the authentic Magisterium of the Bishop of Rome (*LG* 25).

The challenge that Pope Francis's 2020 encyclical poses to everyone, both inside and outside the visible boundaries of the Catholic Church, is not only to engage in promoting its contents and implementing its proposals in our own specific choices and activities. The challenge is also to try and show the validity of its proposals ourselves, through an ever deeper commitment to working *together* and cultivating an ever more effective collaboration, so as to transmit the joy of living and acting as siblings and friends. Finding ways and moments to act in an increasingly *synodal* way—starting with ecclesial structures—will bear witness to the Church's commitment to envisioning, generating, and building a better world.

In *Fratelli Tutti*, Pope Francis's prophetic voice, in the light of the Word of God, reveals the restlessness that characterizes humanity today, but that also inhabits the Church from within. If an ill-concealed concern about an apparently obscure and nebulous future provokes distrust in what is to come, for the Lord's disciples it is lack of faith and hope in the Lord's saving action. The invitation to comprehend the urgency of being "Siblings All" and its concrete implications for building a better world is then a call for each one of us to rediscover courage and zeal, calling back to mind and heart the words and promises of Jesus Christ: "I no longer call you servants, but friends" (Jn 15:15).

APPENDICES

The two appendices are reflections on the two parts of the book. They allow the reader a second look, from a different perspective and in a different style.

Appendix I, "Siblings All after the Pandemic," applies the five criteria for discernment coming from Vatican II to an overwhelming current situation, with the hope of emerging from the COVID-19 health emergency changed for the better!

Appendix II, "Dancing and Mourning," is a scriptural meditation on today's signs of the times, reading Matthew 11:1–19.

The two appendices, coming at the end, serve to round out the reader's comprehension and open new avenues of thought and action. Alternatively, if read before entering into each part of the book, they can serve as helpful if indirect introductions, preparing for the teachings of Vatican II (Part I) and of *Fratelli Tutti* (Part II).

Appendix I

SIBLINGS ALL AFTER THE PANDEMIC

Five principles for transformation in the wake of the global COVID-19 crisis[1]

The global crisis unleashed by the rapid spread of COVID-19 has brought us back to the heart of our human condition, rediscovering a vulnerability to which we had become oblivious, a fragility that remained hidden behind a facade of security that we took for granted. Suddenly we found ourselves exposed, defenseless against an invisible threat, cast into the unknown. Paradoxically, it was the pandemic that opened Pandora's box; by tearing apart the fabric of our daily lives and upending our lifestyles, the pandemic made us experience the limitations of our existence. As if awakened from a fantasy of omnipotence, our eyes opened and, seeing our nakedness (Gen 3:7), we discovered ourselves to be *mortal*.

Perhaps some have perceived the inconsistency of certain options taken by today's globalized culture. Our society prefers to keep the disconcerting drama of death out of plain sight, favoring a private conception of suffering. But this approach has proven incapable of uttering a single word that gives meaning to the drama of the human body wounded by illness.

---

[1] With special reference to Chapter 3 herein.

Moving beyond the restrictions and lockdowns, the temptation is quickly to patch the wound, to fix the cracks as best we can, and to find "fig leaves" with which to cover our nakedness: getting things back to "normal," returning to our usual routine, moving within our habitual horizon as before, trying to quell the existential vertigo into which this crisis has plunged us.

There is, however, the possibility of going another way. We can grasp the "facts" that the pandemic imposed as a crucial epistemological and anthropological turning point.

That is, we can interpret the spread of the pandemic by applying (1) *the criterion of faith*, and recognize in this event a "sign of the times" and an "indication" of the One who comes. The Lord Jesus invites us to look to the "future," rather than quickly reentering the "present."

Looking at the future with the eyes of faith, with the trusting abandonment of children who know themselves to be forever loved, allows us to see this "sign" not as a warning or a dark cloud that threatens slaughter and revenge for the sins of humanity, but as a *kairòs*, a propitious time for reflecting on who we are and who we want to be.

The pandemic becomes, then, a note or marker of truth: we must return to be human again before God the Father, remain human together with the Son made man, and become human in the power of the Holy Spirit, who is Lord and gives life.

This change of direction for humanity is, at the same time, a possibility for conversion for each human being: we are called to abandon the self-centeredness that makes us preoccupied only with ourselves—both as individuals and as a group—in order to embrace an evangelical way of life in which we show ourselves capable of care and concern for others.

This is a change that we owe as much to those who died from the virus as to those who, fighting on the front lines, gave their own lives to save the lives of others. Faith thus leads us to reinterpret life as a gift that can never be taken for granted, and for which we must give an account when we come face to face with God, when the court of or tribunal of history judges our actions and our passage on this earth.

The fear generated by the danger of contagion allowed us to feel an urgent need to become close, to hold our loved ones, to feel as ours the pain of those affected by the virus. A new sense of "we" emerged, bringing us together as human beings beyond our cultural and national differences and helping us see the world as a "common home."

However, this sense of communion and closeness, partly imposed by the emotional wave that swept over us, can easily collapse and quickly fade if it is not supported by strong motivations. Our knack for casual and self-interested relationships can make us quickly forget what the pandemic has revealed to us—that we are made for others, that we need to forge bonds that we can count on.

(2) *Being for others* is part of the process of building our personal identity. It is an indispensable step in acquiring authenticity, not only as people but also as disciples of the Lord. The pandemic, then, represents an experience of "existential exodus" as an invitation to come out of ourselves and as a "paschal entry." We need to transfigure the style of our relationships, moving from the asymmetrical mentality of what is *useful*—in which I bend the other to my own interests—to the harmonic logic of *gratuitousness*—in which I take interest in the other regardless of the benefit that I can derive from them, simply because I recognize their intrinsic value.

Faith also allows us to see the pandemic as an opportunity for deconstructing the mechanisms of indifference of a social system that exists by generating inequality and induces us instead to adopt (3) *the common good as the criterion or measure of private interest*. The emergency has highlighted many contradictions in social coexistence, such as the uninterrupted production of weapons—almost as if it were an essential activity—at the same time that hospitals were lacking basic medical equipment. Or the inequality of the health systems of many countries, where public structures were not able to meet the needs of the weaker and where the right to health was severely compromised. These are countries in which neo-liberal political choices found it convenient to divest from public health, sacrificing prevention and safety in order to increase profit and competitiveness. Such decisions, made with the aim of maximizing capital, now show all their one-sidedness and reveal how the spread of the virus has scarcely been contained, resulting in increased economic, social, and environmental costs that weigh heavily on the health and income of the poorer parts of society.

It is worth noting, however, how the very social resilience of entire nations has been compromised by the inability to contain outbreaks, eventually exposing the more fragile people—the elderly, people with long-term illnesses, and people with disabilities—to a very high risk of mortality.

What has the outbreak of the pandemic taught us? What lessons have we learned from this global phenomenon?

We can try to answer these questions by recalling, first of all, what the Church's social doctrine teaches, namely, that it is not possible to guarantee fundamental human rights without duly promoting the economic and social rights that are fundamental for our coexistence in society. In order to face and effectively manage complex situations such as the pandemic, solutions must be sought on a global scale, laying the foundations for a constructive dialogue among nations and together seeking a common understanding that takes all the relevant variables into account. In this sense, expressing solidarity with the poorer countries and supporting them in the challenges of COVID-19 mean not only helping them to cope with the health crisis by sending vaccines and medical supplies and professional assistance, but also planning broader strategies that allow for a solidarity-based economy and a fairer society to be established.

This pandemic emergency also imposed distancing on us as a preventive measure, making us fear contact and proximity with one another. At a time when culture shows alarming trends toward solipsism and close-mindedness, as evidenced by the unfortunate return of "myopic, extremist, resentful, and aggressive" nationalisms (*FT* 11; 141), we must not let the practice of physical distancing become an emotional attitude or an excuse for running away from the problems of those around us.

To react to the tyranny of ideological tribalism, Pope Francis proposes a "prescription": to dream together to build a better reality (*FT* 8). Refounding ideals starts from identifying a horizon of common meaning, of dreams; this is the antidote to all forms of partisan interests claiming dominance.

In this sense, the Church is called to step forward, combining its (4) *preferential option for the poor* with the healthy *realism that comes from hardworking charity*. Accompanying humanity, gravely wounded by the pandemic, means placing oneself on the side of the last, the broken, the invisible, the abandoned. In doing so, the Church must always be ready to "get its hands dirty," to make its own contribution, leaving room for the creativity of love.

Appearing as a planetary crisis, the pandemic has also highlighted how the common destiny of all human beings is closely linked with the bio-ecological future of the planet. The pandemic crisis thus manifests anew the urgency of (5) *safeguarding creation as a necessity for humanity*.

Factors such as pollution, deforestation, water shortages, soil deterioration and desertification in vast areas of the planet, the depletion of organic matter and soil fertility, the excessive use of chemicals in agriculture, the exorbitant production of waste, the reduction of biodiversity, and climate change have a strong impact on human health. The pandemic has undoubtedly challenged entire populations and forced governments to make choices and plan strategies in response. Decisions, however, always show our true colors: they bring out the values and priorities by which we are guided. So it has become obvious how often keeping an economic system going is considered more important than safeguarding people's health. The same is often true of the health of the environment! The COVID-19 emergency invites us, therefore, to curb the race for wealth at all costs and to rethink the impact of human presence on the planet. If nature is to heal and flourish, and flourish in a way that in turn favors human flourishing, then humans need to respect nature and collaborate with it.

As Pope Francis reminds us: "From this crisis we can come out better or worse. We can slide backward, or we can create something new."[2]

It is time to become aware that countering cultural and ethical deterioration goes hand in hand with taking responsibility for creation. Healing the earth requires healing humans from the evil of selfishness.

---

[2] Pope Francis and Austen Ivereigh, *Let Us Dream: The Path to a Better Future* (London: Simon and Schuster, 2020), 4.

Appendix II

DANCING AND MOURNING

(Mt 11:1–19)

Meditate on the Word to discern in the present

1. A faith attentive to history: The Kingdom of God germinates among the folds of time

When we profess our faith in the Risen Lord who "will come in glory" (Mk 8:38; Lk 9:26), we affirm that as of now it is possible to glimpse the unstoppable unfolding of the Kingdom of God in the folds of time.

The future hope that animates our attachment to Christ does not exempt us from the effort of following in God's footsteps in contemporary history, in order to discover those clues that bear witness to the joyful irruption of the Kingdom of heaven in our present moment. Indeed, the fact of believing always requires the effort to distinguish the Kingdom's traces among the many human facts that would seem to deny that it is already present here.

Jesus urged us to discern the "signs of the times" (Mt 16:3) by which God speaks in contemporary history and, appealing to human conscience, address an invitation to each person to grasp that invisible guiding thread that links what is happening around us to the voice of God who, in secret, speaks from the depths of the heart (Mt 6:6).

In Matthew's Gospel, when the disciples of John the Baptist come to Jesus to ask him why the Twelve do not fast as they and the Pharisees do, he replies: "Can the wedding guests mourn while the bridegroom is with them? But the days will come when the bridegroom will be taken from them, and then they will fast" (Mt 9:15).

Presenting himself as the Bridegroom, Jesus indicates an essential trait in the identity of his disciples: they will have to prove capable of appropriately discerning between the days of "mourning" and the days of "wedding." As his narrative continues, Matthew reports another visit by John the Baptist's disciples to the Lord. They return to ask him about a doubt raised by John himself: "Are you the one who is to come or should we wait for another?" (Mt 11:3). Jesus chose not to answer the question directly, but preferred to reply by pointing to a direction and a fact. He showed that the coming of the Kingdom of God takes place as a transformation of the world: "Go and tell John what you hear and see: the blind regain their sight, the lame walk, lepers are cleansed, the deaf hear, the dead are raised, and the Gospel is proclaimed to the poor" (Mt 11:4–5).

Looking at the earth, paying attention to the conversion and changes taking place on it, they themselves will be able to testify to John the Baptist with the announcement of the Kingdom of God among human beings. Discerning amid what they have seen and heard those signs that Jesus performs by the power of the Holy Spirit, they will be able to narrate how, from the rejoicing of the Bridegroom for his Bride (Isa 62:5), from the exultation of the Father for humanity redeemed from sin, emerges all the beauty of the new creation.

This is the work of God that John the Baptist foretold and that Jesus is now putting into action. For those whose eyes and ears are opened by faith, wherever humanity is healed, restored, and redeemed, it is possible to glimpse the budding of the Kingdom of God.

2.   The doubt of John the Baptist: Jesus points out to each of us our mission in the world

Interestingly, in the midst his hesitancy about Jesus and of his sending his disciples to ask for clarification about his identity, John the Baptist received, by contrast, from Christ's living words, a clarification about his own mission as precursor. Whatever may have been John's doubts about Jesus, Jesus had no doubt about John's role in salvation history.

Addressing the crowd, Jesus explains how John is the prophet of whom the Scriptures had spoken, who came to foretell the beginning of the end times and was sent to prepare the way of the Lord for the redemption of his people (Mt 3:1). Not wishing to leave any room for misunderstanding, he declares even more explicitly that "among those born of a woman there has never arisen anyone greater than John the Baptist" (Mt 11:11a).

The expression "born of a woman" is typically Semitic (Job 11:12; Sir 10:18; Gal 4:4) and can be understood here as a counterpoint to the title "Son of Man" (Num 23:19; Job 25:6; Ps 8:4), which Jesus would attribute to himself (Mt 11:19) a little later.

In Matthew's narrative, Jesus uses it several times to gradually introduce his disciples to an understanding of his mission as "the Lord's Anointed," as the One sent by the Father "to serve and to give his life as a ransom for many" (Mt 20:28).

John is proclaimed as the greatest of all the prophets, even compared to Moses (Deut 34:10–12), and yet Jesus observes that "the least in the kingdom of heaven is greater than he" (Mt 11:11b). In reporting such a stunning comparison, there can be little doubt that it is an authentic expression of Jesus. The evangelist Matthew emphasizes the superabundance of the economy of fulfillment, over and above the promise contained in the Law and the Prophets; through Christ, the true little one of the Kingdom (Lk 9:48), humanity marks the passage "from this world to the Father" (Jn 13:1), from the earthly reality of "siblings born of women" to the ultimate reality of the "sons and daughters of God."

Jesus clarifies John's identity by referring back to his own. He lets us sense how the good news that he came to proclaim to us brings truth to each of us, shedding light on our mission as disciples. While the mystery of his person remains an ineffable and inexhaustible mystery for everyone, in placing our lives before him we have a way to understand ourselves more fully as well as what the Father calls us to so that we can contribute to the building of the Kingdom. With humility we must go to Jesus and ask him, "Who are you?" And showing us the human face of the Son beloved from eternity, he will tell us who we are for him. As he invites us to follow him ever more closely, Jesus reveals our true identity. For baptized persons, walking the road that leads to discovering the truth about themselves coincides with setting out on the "holy journey" (Ps 83:6) that leads to embracing the mission that the Lord points out. The teaching of Vatican II rings true to this day: with simplicity and wisdom the Council reminds us that "Christ, the final Adam, by the revelation of the mystery of the Father and His love, fully reveals man to man himself and makes his supreme calling clear" (*GS* 22).

3.   The "violent" and the "meek": Two opposite ways of being and acting

By comparing "the greatest among those born of women" to "the least in the Kingdom" (Mt 11:11), Jesus draws attention to the ways that the Gospel overturns human logic. This anticipates the teaching on "evangelical greatness" that the evangelist will develop more explicitly in the last part of his Gospel.

Matthew relates that Jesus, seeing the hour of his end approaching, admonished his disciples, saying: "Whoever wishes to become great among you shall be your servant" (Mt 20:26). He invites them not to conform to the common mentality, to the criteria by which society evaluates someone's success and prestige, but to discern according to a new criterion that can be understood only in the light of his Paschal Mystery: "The last shall be first and the first shall be last" (Mt 20:16).

In the Kingdom of heaven, those who have made themselves "last" in imitation of the Son of Man, in humble service and generous self-giving, will be considered "first," while those who dominate others and insistently affirm themselves, who strive to occupy places of honor and receive people's admiration, will be judged "last" (Mt 20:16).

After clarifying the identity of John the Baptist, the paradox of evangelical "greatness" is evoked in the image of "the violent who take 'the Kingdom of heaven by force'" (Mt 11:12). This we understand as the antithesis of the "poor in spirit" (Mt 5:3) and the "meek" (Mt 5:5) who will inherit the earth.

Here, the Gospel seems to suggest that there are two mutually opposing attitudes of dealing with contemporary history and of disposing oneself to receiving Christ's message: as violent or as children of God (Mt 5:9).

The former mistake power for strength and face the present with the sole concern of providing for their own needs, even at the cost of ignoring the suffering and pain that their actions and omissions cause in their fellow human.

The latter, on the other hand, know how to recognize, in the wounds and vulnerability of their contemporaries, and in the helplessness of those who suffer all kinds of injustice and abuse, the face of Christ humbled on the Cross.

By taking upon themselves the human burden of the weakest, they respond to the Lord's words: "Whatever you did for one of the least of these brothers and sisters of mine, you did for me" (Mt 25:40).

God's judgment on history and the newness that the Kingdom of God represents in history cannot be understood without taking on the radical teaching of Jesus on the paradox of "evangelical greatness."

For us, Jesus's teaching becomes a warning always to keep in mind and not to neglect in our pastoral action. We must escape the temptation to make use of worldly power and reject the illusory belief that the effectiveness of our mission depends on such power. It is not the means that make the proclamation of the Gospel greater, stronger, or more convincing, but the faith we place in God and in the life-giving dynamism of his Word.

The Apostle Paul, when he finds himself lacking, testifies to his full confidence in the manifold grace of God coming to his rescue: "My grace is sufficient for you, for my power is made perfect in weakness" (2 Cor 12:9). Recognizing the frailty and insufficiency of his human condition does not frighten Paul but spurs him on to trust even more in Christ's promises.

In this way, Paul can affirm that Christian greatness comes from God and no human source, that it is based on the manifestation of God and not on the persuasiveness of wise talk (1 Cor 2:3–4). Drawing on his own experience, Paul can attest that "we have this treasure in jars of clay to show that this all-surpassing power is from God and not from us" (2 Cor 4:7).

4.   The lament and the dance: The parable of the obstinate children

We read the parable of the stubborn children as an enigmatic text that lends itself to multiple levels of reading. Its evocative style, suggestive of several meanings, does not allow for an unambiguous interpretation. Saint Jerome pointed out the difficulty the Fathers of the Church had in agreeing on an exegesis of these verses.[1]

Nevertheless, we can try to grasp its meaning and offer a brief commentary by paying attention to the question with which Jesus introduces it: "To what can I compare this generation?" (Mt 11:16).

With this question Jesus refers back to prophetic books, especially the preaching of Jeremiah (Jer 6:10–15) that firmly denounces the people's resistance to God's calls. Jesus addresses his contemporaries and points to their hardness of heart, their steadfast stubbornness in opposing God's will. They have refused God's invitation as much to conversion as to joy.

---

[1] Jerome, *Commentary on Matthew*, 2.11.16.

From the space of play, Jesus borrows the image of a children's game that consists of mimicking the basic realities of life: dancing at a wedding and mourning a death. We can almost imagine the scene of those children on the square, intent on having fun together. Some improvise as musicians, making the sounds of flutes and cymbals, inviting the others to dance to the rhythm of their singing, now sad, now festive. However, others refuse to play along, ignore their invitations, forcing them to protest in exasperation: "We played the flute for you, and you did not dance; we wailed, and you did not mourn!" (Mt 11:17).

Jesus says that "this generation" is like the children in the parable, because it has not been drawn into God's delightful love and has not responded to his desire to enter into relationship. It has rejected John's lament, declining his call to repentance, to return to God, but it has also rejected the joyful proclamation of the Son of Man, who revealed the coming of the Kingdom as a wedding feast (Mt 22:1–14).

The inability to distinguish properly between the days of "mourning" and the days of "wedding" has led "this generation" to discredit John, because "he neither eats nor drinks," and to mock Jesus for the exact opposite, because "he is a glutton and a drunkard" (Mt 11:19). This generation finds fault with both, because its heart is closed and its ear deaf to the calls of the Holy Spirit.

Instead, this generation should be dressed in mourning with John and then put on the wedding garment with Jesus, since the Baptist's invitation to conversion was preparation for the wedding feast of the Lamb (Rev 19:7).

Jesus laments the resistance of those of his own generation who did not accept God's game. Believing themselves to be self-sufficient, they refused the offer of forgiveness, unlike the publicans and sinners who recognized their sin and accepted the invitation to conversion, becoming friends of the Bridegroom.

Jesus denouncing the behavior of his contemporaries is not to be understood legally as a sentence of guilt. He means it as a work of wisdom (Mt 11:19): it is an act of love, like the sound of a lover lamenting over an unfaithful spouse (Ezek 16:44–52) or the reproach of a parent who has at heart the growth and flourishing of a "stubborn and rebellious" child (Deut 21:18–21).

The Lord addresses the crowds today, as he did then, with his heartfelt call to make room for salvation. We need to feel challenged by his words, to recognize ourselves as members of that generation he rebuked for their obstinacy in turning away from the newness of God's Kingdom and from the signs that accompany it.

Jesus also asks us to change our mentality and not to fall into that lethargic spirit, that lukewarm faith, which makes the heart insensitive to God's warnings in contemporary history.

The pandemic is like the "song of lamentation" that echoes in our time and urges us today to go along with God's "game." In this difficult situation with its tragic implications for so many siblings all, we have the responsibility to get in tune with God, to move toward the suffering, to find the right rhythm with God.

In order to show our fidelity to the Lord Jesus, it is necessary to adhere to the present, to recognize it as a propitious occasion in which to allow ourselves to be reached by his mercy. We need to withdraw from listlessness, apathy, and laziness. We need to show that our faith is capable of generous responses, effective charity, concrete solidarity.

This virus is teaching us that, in spite of the many advances made by science, the unpredictability of various circumstances shakes what may seem to be unshakable certainties, revealing the insufficiency and fallibility of our human means.

Though it is true that there are certain incurable diseases in this world, it is even truer that no patient is eternally incurable. Jesus is the supreme Physician of souls and bodies, and the unfailing cure that he prescribes is Christian love. Like "balm" (Jer 51:3) and the "oil of gladness" (Isa 61:3), this love heals all wounds, especially those of the soul. Let us pour it out abundantly on our afflicted siblings, especially on those most affected by the effects of the pandemic and who have lost hope, those who are lonely and embittered.

By our gestures of care, by the love that God spreads through us, the world will recognize that we are disciples of the Risen Lord (Jn 13:34). Because where the human flourishes, there is manifested the joy of the Bridegroom.

INDEX

Made in United States
Troutdale, OR
06/23/2023

10748611R00136